SO-ADO-608

Children of Zion

CHILDREN

of

ZION

HENRYK GRYNBERG

Translated from the Polish by Jacqueline Mitchell
With an Afterword by Israel Gutman

NORTHWESTERN UNIVERSITY PRESS

Evanston, Illinois

Northwestern University Press
Evanston, Illinois 60208-4210

First published in Polish in 1994 under the title *Dzieci Syjonu* by
Wydawnictwo Karta, Warsaw. Copyright © 1994 by Henryk Grynberg.
English translation published 1997 by arrangement with the author. Copy-
right © 1997 by Northwestern University Press. All rights reserved.

Printed in the United States of America

ISBN 0-8101-1353-8 (cloth)
ISBN 0-8101-1354-6 (paper)

Library of Congress Cataloging-in-Publication Data

Grynberg, Henryk.
    [Dzieci Syjonu. English]
    Children of Zion / Henryk Grynberg ; translated from the Polish by
Jacqueline Mitchell ; with an afterword by Israel Gutman.
        p. cm. — (Jewish lives)
    ISBN 0-8101-1353-8 (cloth : alk. paper). — ISBN 0-8101-1354-6
(paper : alk. paper)
    1. Jewish children—Poland—Interviews. 2. Jewish children in the
Holocaust—Poland—Interviews. 3. Refugees, Jewish—Soviet Union—
Interviews. 4. Poland—Ethnic relations. 5. Soviet Union—Ethnic rela-
tions. I. Title. II. Series.
DS135.P63G8413 1998
940.53'18—dc21   97-39677
                                                            CIP

The paper used in this publication meets the minimum requirements of the
American National Standard for Information Sciences—Permanence of
Paper for Printed Library Materials, ANSI Z39.48-1984.

*To the memory of the fathers, mothers, and children
whose bones marked the ways and stations of torture in the inhuman
expanses of Eastern Europe, Siberia, and Central Asia*

❁

Contents

✤

Preface

The documentary tale *Children of Zion* consists of fragments of interview records compiled in Palestine in 1943 by the Polish Centrum Informacji na Wschód (Eastern Center for Information) on the basis of the testimony of Jewish children evacuated from the Soviet Union to Palestine. These documents, entitled *The Palestinian Protocols*, were sent to London, to Stanisław Kot, minister of information and documentation of the Polish government-in-exile. Copies are in the archives of the Hoover Institution at Stanford University, in the collection "Poland—Ministry of Information and Documentation," box 197, folders 1–4, "Polish Information Center—Jerusalem, Reports of Jewish Deportees." I thank Norman Naimark, Lucjan Śniadower, and Hanna Cudna-Martyniuk for bringing these documents to my attention and making them available to me.

From *The Palestinian Protocols*, which describe first the atrocities of the German occupiers in 1939 and then the fate of the refugees and deportees in the Soviet Union, a classic modern tragedy emerges in which—according to Jolanta Brach-Czaina's definition of this kind of tragedy—helpless, anonymous victims perish in a manner "unconnected with their own actions or beliefs" and "without the possibility of resisting the evil" (*Szczeliny Istnienia*, Warsaw, 1992). These documents are more credible than others, because in general children do not manipulate information.

The instructions to the questionnaire filled out by the refugees make it clear that the Polish authorities in exile wanted "to show the world . . . that Jews in Soviet Russia, because of the unofficial antisemitism there . . . suffered

twice—as Polish citizens and as Jews." But the testimony of
the Jewish children does not corroborate this. It also contradicts the position of the Polish Eastern Command—a position to which Krystyna Kersten inclines in her book *Polacy,
Żydzi, Kommunizm*—that in the case of Polish citizens after
the amnesty, the NKVD (People's Commisariat of Internal
Affairs, a predecessor of the KGB) deliberately made it easier
for Jews to leave the camps and other places of exile, while
making it more difficult for ethnic Poles. Herling-Grud-
ziński's *A World Apart* contradicts this position as well.

Only 871 Jewish children were rescued from the inferno
out of all the Polish children evacuated to Iran in 1942, whose
total number is estimated at between twelve and twenty thou-
sand, even though Jews accounted for 30 to 50 percent of Polish citizens exiled and deported to the Russian interior. (Jan
Tomasz Gross and Irena Grudzińska-Gross in their book
*War Through Children's Eyes: The Soviet Occupation of
Poland and the Deportations, 1939–1941* put the number of
Polish children evacuated at not quite twenty thousand, and
Kersten at twelve to fourteen thousand.) In similar dispropor-
tion, out of the 130 children's documents from the Hoover
Institution archive cited in the Polish edition of the Grosses'
book (120 in the English version), there were only four testi-
monies of Jewish children.

To improve the narrative and rid the language of the reports of its wooden, bureaucratic style, I have had to recast
most sentences and paragraphs. However, the contents remain
unchanged. Each paragraph represents a separate voice. I have
tried to retain the special character of that rare synthesis of
child's narration and official report. Some lesser-known geo-
graphical names were distorted in the protocols. Many of
them I managed to identify and correct, but perhaps not all.

The text is taken from seventy-three testimonies, a list of
which appears at the end of the book. (Two of them, nos. 119
and 175, were given by the same person, apparently on two
separate occasions, and they complement each other.) The age
range of the children is significant: from eleven to eighteen,
but the majority were thirteen or fourteen. To complete the

picture I have added fragments from the testimony of a twen-ty-five-year-old woman from Limanowa (no. 163 in the list) and one sentence from a twenty-five-year-old "soldier's wife" (no. 88) who had arranged a marriage of convenience. My job was mainly one of selecting and arranging. Too much hap-pened to require any fabrication on my part, and I feel that the epic described here demonstrates the boundless potential of "documentary prose."

Headnotes by Zeev Schuss provide the historical back-ground to the testimony of the children.

Henryk Grynberg
Franklin Park, Virginia
1993

Children of Zion

We Lived Pretty Well

My father bought hay in the countryside and carted it to Warsaw and other cities. We had our own house, and we were doing well.

My father leased orchards in the Czerniaków area and sold the fruit to Warsaw.

My father dealt in cattle. He had squires and peasants for customers.

My father was a cattle trader. We lived in a house of our own, and we did pretty well.

My father had a dairy in Czarny Dunajec, where there were one hundred Jewish families, and they all made a good living.

My father owned a mill.

My father was a timber grader. His job was to survey forests for logging.

My father was a forest manager. We had a three-floor apartment building in Biłgoraj, opposite the convent.

My father had an estate near Łuniniec. Forty-five thousand acres with a sawmill and a carpenter's shop. But we lived in Warsaw.

My father was a shoemaker and had two apprentices. His customers were rich country squires and government officials.

My father owned a shoe factory where twenty people worked.

My father owned a textile mill at 220 Piotrkowska Street which employed more than a hundred workers. We lived in Łódź.

My father owned a candle factory and a wholesale food warehouse. We lived in Różan.

My father managed a brewery in partnership with my uncle. Our house was near the brewery in the factory district of Tarnów.

My father was a wealthy man. We had an apartment building and a wholesale flour warehouse in Wieliczka.

My father had a paper warehouse in Jarosław—the only one in the whole region.

My father had warehouses for raw wool, and we were among the richest Jews in Majdan.

My father owned a tavern; my parents never complained that they were doing badly.

My father owned a bus that ran between Stoczek and Łuków.

My father was a chauffeur.

My father had a little store. We lived in our own house, and we lived pretty well.

My father had a machine that made hosiery. My sister and my older brother helped him, and I went to school.

My father was a cashier in a factory. My sisters, sixteen-year-old Helka and fifteen-year-old Irka, were studying to get good jobs because my father did not earn enough.

My father worked in the office at Stock and Company. I and my older sister Gerda went to grammar school.

My father was a bookkeeper for the National Canned Goods Factory.

My father was a *shoykhet*,[*] and we had a kosher meat stall. The older children didn't work; they went to school.

My father was a *shoykhet*, and we had our own house. There were five children; we all went to school, and we didn't lack for anything.

My father was a famous rabbi. He had many followers in Siedlce, and they bought him a house. In it was the *beys medresh*[†] full of valuable books and our private apartment.

---

[*]Man who slaughters animals for kosher meat according to Jewish ritual law.
[†]Study house connected with a synagogue.

My grandfather was a rabbi in Leżajsk. Because he was very old and could not perform all his duties, my father used to substitute for him.

My father was a religious man and owned a candy factory. He was one of the most respected citizens in Jarosław.

My father was a frail man. He had a bad heart and did nothing but study all day long. We lived off what our relatives in America sent us.

My father made leather goods. He ran a workshop with several workers, and we did pretty well.

My father was a hatmaker, and we lived pretty well. We had a stall in the market and a workshop at home where my father made caps and hats.

My father was a tanner and made a good living.

My father manufactured brushes. We were never rich.

My father was a cabinetmaker, and we lived in a house of our own near Leżajsk.

My father was a cabinetmaker. My mother died when I was three and my father remarried. But my stepmother was like a mother to me.

My parents had a clothing store. We lived in Warsaw.

My father was a baker, and we lived in Oświęcim.* We had our own bakery and a baked goods store in the marketplace, and we lived a quiet life.

My father owned a haberdashery in Kraków. A year before the war we moved to Rozwadów when we got an inheritance there from my grandfather.

We had a haberdashery in Cologne. In 1938 the Germans deported us and we spent a long time in a camp near Zbąszyn. My father died there, and my mother and I moved to Rozwadów, where we had relatives.

In 1939 I was living in Warsaw at a yeshiva boarding school, where I studied.

My father was a bookkeeper. He knew politics and predicted that there would be a war with Germany.

---

*Auschwitz.

We lived in Bielsko-Biała, on Kościuszko Street. My father worked for a lawyer. He was a lieutenant in the reserves and every year he was called up for exercises. Two weeks before war broke out, my father went to the office and there he got his orders for immediate mobilization. He didn't even have time to say good-bye to us.

Two weeks before war broke out, my parents sent me from Kraków to Przemyśl because they suspected that the Germans would be coming.

Ten days before war broke out, orders were given to evacuate Bielsko. We weren't allowed to take much luggage with us on the train, and we arrived in Lwów almost without a thing. We got an apartment on Third of May Street, but my father didn't know what to do next because we did not have much money saved.

A week before war broke out, we left Nowy Sącz, which was not far from the border, and went to my grandfather's in Rozwadów.

We fled Przasnysz and went to Pułtusk because my father expected war to break out and my stepmother was about to give birth.

The Jews fled Pułtusk, but we stayed behind, because Mama was weak and my father was afraid to leave the house with the young children.

One day when I was playing with the other children, I saw sheets of paper being pasted on the walls. I could not read yet, and I ran to Mama and asked her to see what it was. When Mama came back, many people were standing there, and the word was that there would be war. My father came home very worried. He said that everyone was getting out and who knew whether we'd be able to get a cart.

Before war broke out, my father went to Łuck, to his brother's, and Mama sold off the clothes in the store.

A few days before war broke out, people in the town were saying that danger was approaching, and my father began to travel from village to village asking for the money they owed him for cattle. But very few paid up, and my father was left almost penniless.

I was eight years old and I went to elementary school in Kałuszyn. My father escaped to Brześć.

Two days before war broke out, we left Bielsko and went to my grandfather's in Grzymałów.

Bielsko was on the border; many Germans lived with us and were always threatening the Jews, so Mama packed our things and we fled. My oldest brother, Abram, was fifteen at the time, and my younger sisters, Marta and Róża, were ten and eight.

Soldiers were being massed in Różan, and orders were given to evacuate civilians, so my family escaped to Długo-siodło, where we had relatives.

When they ordered the evacuation of Różan, we escaped to Długosiodło, where we met Jews from many other border towns.

When they ordered the evacuation, we escaped to Ostrów Mazowiecka, where a cousin of ours lived.

❋

When War Broke Out

On the night of August 23 to 24, 1939, at a state dinner in the Kremlin, two international agreements were signed between the foreign ministers of Nazi Germany and the Soviet Union, Joachim von Ribbentrop and Vyacheslav Molotov. The first was a nonaggression pact, which was made public. The other was a secret agreement that, in the event of political or territorial changes in Poland, the border between the German and Soviet areas of influence would run along the Rivers Narew, Vistula, and San. A week later, on September 1, Germany attacked Poland from the west and the south and quickly occupied a large part of its territory. When Poland's defeat became apparent, the Red Army invaded from the east on September 17 and captured vast areas of Polish territory, beyond what Molotov and Ribbentrop had agreed. On September 28 a new agreement was signed in Moscow between Nazi Germany and the Soviet Union. Now the border between the German- and Soviet-occupied areas was established as following the Rivers Pisa, Narew, Bug, Vistula, and San. On October 4 yet another agreement was signed, between Molotov and the German ambassador in Moscow, Friedrich W. Schulenburg. This final agreement determined that the border would run along the Ostrołęka–Treblinka line and from there along the Bug River south to Brest-Litovsk and west to the San River above Jarosław, and to the Polish-Hungarian border. Certain Polish settlements near the new border changed hands several times.

Across the new border in the eastern part of Poland lived a mixed population of over 13 million Poles, Ukrainians, Byelorussians, Lithuanians, Jews, and others. Polish government censuses estimated the number of Jews in these territories at more than 1.3 million.

When the bulletins were posted saying that the Germans had attacked Poland, there was panic in our town and people started to run away. But my father did not want to abandon the house.

On Friday, September 1, German planes bombed Oświęcim. A bomb fell right near us and killed three people. People started to run away. A cart with two horses was already standing in front of our house, but the army was stationed in town and they needed bread to be baked. The soldiers said that they would defend the town and there was no reason to run away.

On Friday, September 1, panic broke out. Poles, Jews, anyone who could was running away in the direction of Lwów. My father did not want to run away. How could he just set off into the wide world with six children and no money? Besides, he believed that the Polish army would mount an effective resistance. But when people began saying that the Germans were already in Podhajce and that the last train was about to leave, my father changed his mind. There was a terrible crush on the train. There was no place to sit or stand. People were walking on top of people; children were trampled. New passengers got on at every station, and fights broke out between the newcomers and those who were already there. When airplanes approached, the train would stop and people would trample over each other to jump out and take cover in ditches. When the air raid was over, they would cram themselves back into the train, losing relatives and belongings in the process. All the while you could hear shrieking from people who had been robbed, children crying, people shouting. For two days and nights we traveled like this to Lwów. People said Lwów would be defended, that a big battle would be fought there. Trenches were dug; even old Jews with *peyes*[*] helped to dig.

On the day war broke out, people ran every which way, not knowing what to do. The rabbi was so worried that he sent us home. And yet, on Sunday I went to *kheyder*[†] as

---

[*]Sidecurls worn by many Orthodox Jewish men and boys.
[†]Religious school for children.

usual. Not many of the students were there, but the class did take place. All of a sudden we heard terrible crashing sounds, and we saw that the ceiling was on fire. The teacher ordered us to jump out the window one after the other. We wanted to run home, but the rabbi would not let us, because the sky was black with airplanes, and he took us to a brick house that had a shelter. That day, our house burned down with all our belongings, and my father said, Why should we risk our lives in town?—better to hide in the countryside. We moved into a peasant's barn. With a few bricks he built us a stove, on which Mama cooked potatoes. But before Rosh Hashana my father was summoned, because the town had no *shoykhet*. And so we returned to Tomaszów and lived with relatives.

On Friday, September 1, the yeshiva students fled to their families, but I could not get away because the train line to Różan had been cut off.

When we heard shots being fired, we packed up our things and took cover in the shelter. A few hours later, the Polish authorities gave orders to leave the town, but the train station had been bombed and we had to go to Nowy Targ on foot. They bombed the train, and it took us three days to get to Podhorce, where we had friends.

When war broke out, I was with Mama on vacation in Falenica. When the Germans bombed the orphanage in Otwock and killed many children, we left everything behind and took the train back to Warsaw. The dark city made a terrible impression on us, and I was afraid I would lose Mama.

When war broke out, we were in an orchard near Skolimów, and we returned to Warsaw on foot. We found the apartment open, robbed. In our neighborhood the most bombs fell and the most people died.

My uncle had gone to Warsaw to pick up some merchandise; the day he was coming back, war broke out. The train was bombed near Garwolin, and my uncle returned on foot, with his arm wounded. He advised us to leave Chełm, where there were armaments factories. On Saturday evening we got onto the cart with Grandpa and Grandma, uncles and aunts and their children—eleven people in all. The road was littered with broken-down cars and dead horses. The German planes dove down low and shot at people. We took cover in ditches and heard the groaning of the wounded, whom no one was interested in.

On Saturday, September 2, the Germans bombed Limanowa.

On Saturday morning my father came back from synagogue very upset and told us that people were saying the Germans were on their way to Rabka. Mama left everything on the stove and packed up the cushions. She gave a little suitcase to my brother Meir, who was twelve years old, and gave me a small bundle. All the Jews were running away, and only a few old men who were unable to travel stayed behind. There were so many people on the road with bundles on their shoulders, so many horse-drawn carts and cars, that we were able to reach Wiśniowiec only with difficulty. There, my father hired a cart, which cost us a lot of money, but after driving for a few hours the peasant said he was not going any further and told us to get off. My father begged him to take pity on the children. Mama cried, but it was no use. He pushed us off the cart and went on his way. My father did not have the strength to carry the bedding, so he threw it down by the side of the road, and Mama threw away the suitcase. We got to Rzeszów, and the next day boarded a train for Jarosław.

The Germans bombed Wyszków just one day after war broke out. People were jumping out the windows of burning houses.

On Saturday, the second day of war, the bombing of Siedlce began. Piękna Street, where the finest stores were and where the rich Jews lived, was completely burned down. Kozia Street too, where the craftsmen had their shops.

The Germans bombed Siedlce for days and days. The reconnaissance planes would fly in at eight in the morning, then at nine the bombers would come; the bombing raid would last until eleven. Then again after lunch. The town was on fire. People escaped to the countryside and lay down in the fields or under trees, because the cellars were becoming graveyards. Twenty-five hundred dead were counted in the space of ten days. On Saturday, September 9, at nine in the morning, we ran out of the house like the others and hid in the trenches that had been dug for protection. When we got back, we no longer had a roof over our heads. Everything we owned had been burned, along with all the books and mementos that had been passed down from generation to generation. The damage was worst in the streets where Jews lived. We saw the army running away. Many civilians, especially younger people, were also running away. We took shelter in a house that had survived and thought fearfully about the next day.

German planes bombed the railway station in Mrozy, then our town the following day. One bomb landed near the church and killed thirty-two Jews who were standing on line for bread. I recognized six-year-old Mendele among the dead. Fires were breaking out everywhere. My father took me by the hand and we ran to the ice cream factory, which was a brick building outside of town. But soon we had to escape again, because even there the fire was getting close. Then I lost my father, and all night I sat out in the open with my brother Abram. All of Kałuszyn was on fire, and it was as bright as day. Children were crying from hunger, and one Jew ran to a village and brought us some bread. In his arms he had a baby a few months old whose mother had died. On the third day we went to see what was left of our house. We saw black chimneys. The stench was terrible. Many horses and cows had been burned alive in the barns. Many old and sick people had not managed to escape. Next to the stream that flowed there, we could recognize the spot where our house had stood. We went through the rubble, and Abram cried out in joy because he had found the sewing machine. It was a new machine and represented our father's entire fortune. We also found a few cooking pots. While we were raking through the rubble of our house, my father arrived, in tears, because he had just found out that our grandfather had perished in the fire. Grandfather was eighty years old and blind, and he lived on the upper floor. His remains were found in the charred rubble. A few brick houses on Warszawska Street had survived, and the synagogue. All the homeless people took shelter there; the crush of people was terrible, and the children cried all the time.

When our house in Kałuszyn burned down, we went to live with a peasant outside the town; Mama gave birth there. The peasants brought us milk, potatoes, and kasha. Mama cried for days on end.

The bombing of Brok lasted a whole day, and most of the houses burned down. On our street only one house survived.

When they started to bomb Goworowo, we fled to the countryside and wandered for a few days. But on Saturday my father decided to go back home.

The battle for Różan lasted three days and three nights, and the town was so completely destroyed that there was no point in going back.

In Lwów people were saying that there would not be any war, and that they would let us off with a scare. So when the alarm came everyone thought it was just a test, and several thousand people died before they could reach the shelters.

In Mielec there were airplane and munitions factories that employed several thousand workers, but not a single Jew. The workers were terrible antisemites and they poisoned the atmosphere in the town. The Germans bombed the town for a few days; then came a concentrated air raid on a munitions factory, and seventy people died. The next day twenty people from the factory were shot for passing information to the enemy, among them the manager and the foremen. One of them had been caught up a tree at night, signaling to the planes.

When the bombing of the convent began, we fled to the other end of Biłgoraj to our uncle's. The heaviest air raid was on Monday, September 4. When he heard the news that the synagogue and the *beys medresh* were on fire, my father ran to see what had become of our house, and he found it in flames. Out of several hundred houses only twenty survived.

Our town was bombed on September 8. Fourteen airplanes took part in the bombing. Three thousand people lived in Nachal.

Twelve hundred Jews lived in Izbica. The bombing began in the second week of war.

One hundred fifty Jews lived in Krzeszów. The Poles took up positions in nearby Stalowa Wola and fired on the Germans from Mount Frycz. In order to see them better, they burned our town down.

Not far from our house and the brewery there was a munitions factory that was a target for bombing, and bombs fell on our house.

When our house was bombed, we went to live with our aunt on Gęsia Street. Before Rosh Hashana, when Mama was getting ready to go to synagogue, the bombing started up again, and Auntie's house burned down. We went to a cousin's on Pańska Street. The food situation kept getting worse, and Mama cried because she had no bread for us. One day my father came back with a lot of bread. We ate that bread for three days.

During the bombing of Warsaw, we sat in the cellar day after day and night after night. Mama would not let my father go out for food. She said it was better for the children to be hungry than to lose their father. Then a bomb shattered a canned goods factory and we went and took cans of sardines, pickles, and tomatoes. The worst thing was when there was no water. People went to the Vistula River, and many did not come back.

A week after war broke out, when the order came for all the men to leave Warsaw, we traveled by horse to Brześć and from there by train to Łuniniec. One day before the Russians arrived, we were advised to abandon our property, but my father did not know where to escape to. The officers who came to our house were apathetic and disoriented, and the trains did not know what direction to go in. We went by cart to Sarny.

Mr. Bluman, the owner of the firm where my father worked, managed to get some gasoline from somewhere and took us out of Warsaw in his car. We drove the whole night to

get to Lublin, on a road swarming with refugees. Because the
government was in Lublin, the Germans bombed the town
terribly, and we had to take shelter in the fields. We set off
with the army toward the Romanian border, but we made
such slow progress that we never managed to cross it.

The Germans bombed our town terribly, so we hired a cart
and departed. We saw lots of refugees. Carts were clogging up
the road; new cars stood abandoned for lack of gas. Three
days later we arrived in Dubienka, where Mama's father lived.

Day after day they bombed our town, so we loaded our
things onto a cart and started on our way. But just outside
town the army commandeered our cart and we had to go on
foot with our bundles on our backs. The soldiers chased us
off the highway, saying that our bundles were like signals to
the German planes. We trudged into Bochnia at one in the
morning. The next morning the planes returned. They dipped
down low, dropped incendiary bombs, and fired machine
guns. We hid in a bombed-out house. When things died down,
my father bought a horse and cart, and we moved on. But we
did not know where to go: whatever place we got to, the Germans immediately closed in, as if they were hunting us down.

We could not get a cart, because the army had requisi-
tioned all the horses. But the soldiers were kind and they let
us onto their carts. One cart was so loaded down with food
that it could take only three children, so I was put on another
one while Mama ran behind. During the night the cart turned
down a side road, and in the morning I found that I was
alone. Planes had suddenly appeared. They were flying so
low that I could see people sitting in them. The soldiers scattered into the woods while I covered myself with a tarpaulin;
I thought to myself that it would be better for them to kill me
than for me to be left all alone. Then I ran down the roads
crying. Soldiers took me onto their cart and said perhaps I
would find Mama in Kraków. I did not find Mama in
Kraków, but I did meet our neighbors who had also fled from
Bielsko. Kraków was being shelled, so we went to Wisznica.
After that, all the roads were cut off, and we were told to hide
in a cellar.

❁

Germans, Germans, Germans

*During the short time that the German army held the Polish territories it
had initially occupied — before handing part of them over to the Soviets — German soldiers of the Wehrmacht and the SS persecuted the Jews
in a way that foreshadowed what was in store. This is when the forced
exile of the Jewish population from the German- to the Soviet-occupied
zone began. When the Soviets returned a number of Polish settlements to
German hands, many Jews there preferred to abandon their towns and
follow the Red Army into the Soviet-occupied zone.*

*In order to "solve" the problem of the numerous refugees and dis-
placed persons in the vicinity of the new border, the Germans and Soviets agreed to repatriate the displaced population, and the border was
briefly opened to refugees. However, the Germans did not allow Jewish
refugees to return to their homes.*

A week after war broke out, my aunt ran in screaming that
the Germans were coming. We were terrified: we had never
imagined they were so near. My father, who was a religious
man and wore a beard, was afraid to remain in the town, and
he fled to Łańcut. A few hours later we heard a knock on our
door. Uncle Leib opened up and in came five Germans. They
asked who the owner was. My uncle answered that the owner
had fled. "And why haven't *you* fled?" shouted one of the
Germans. He began lashing us with his riding crop. Then he
asked where other Jews were living. My brother managed to
sneak out the side door and warn the neighbors, so when the
Germans left our house they saw Jews running across the
fields in the direction of town. They fired but didn't hit any-

one. Then the Germans gave the order that by six in the evening not a single Jew was to remain in the village. If they came upon one, they would shoot on the spot. So we quickly packed our things and fled to Łańcut.

My mother was baking bread when the bombing began. She left everything, and we fled to the forest. The next day the Germans arrived in Izbica—three tanks and lots of motorcycles. Everyone went into hiding. There was not a living soul on the street except the *shoykhet,* Chaim Falek, who was shutting the door of his house. The Germans shot and killed him. Then they called all the men out and ordered them to stand with their hands up. After an hour an officer appeared. He noticed one of Josek's sons, who was very tall. The whole family was tall. They were the most popular in town. The officer shot and wounded that giant of a boy. He was taken to the hospital in Zamość, but he died. The whole town mourned him. Among the Germans there were some Austrian soldiers, who comforted us by saying that the Russians would soon be coming.

The German planes bombed the railway station first, then two days later the Jewish quarter. So we got out of Łuków and went to Stoczek. Six days later the Germans drove into Stoczek. They pounded on the doors and shouted, *"Juden heraus!"* When we came out they ordered us to line up in rows. Several Jews were shot on the spot, while the rest were ordered to pack up a few essentials and leave the town, which they burned after our departure.

The Germans bombed Stoczek Łukowski on the seventh of September. The planes flew very low and dropped incendiary bombs, so the fires could not be put out. Mama fled with us to the village of Gizubka, but our father stayed behind. On September 12 we saw the glow of a huge fire, then on the following morning crowds of people. They had escaped from our town, and our father was among them. He told us that the Germans had set fire to all the houses and had not allowed anyone to rescue their belongings. We went to Łuków.

All through the night we could hear shots, and the next morning we heard Germans shouting the order for all Jews to

come out of hiding; if not, they would be shot. Mr. Wolf came
out. They also took Mrs. Wolf's brother Abram. In the evening, when the other men were returning home, Mrs. Wolf
ran off to look for her husband and brother. I ran after her.
We found them by the church, along with other dead Jews.
There were dead soldiers lying there too—they were said to
have been Jewish prisoners of war. The square was red with
blood. I saw it with my own eyes. I heard the wailing and the
weeping. The Germans did not allow the bodies to be
claimed. A small group of prominent Jews went to the general and got his permission, but the Germans at the church
would not believe this and threatened to shoot a hundred
more Jews if it turned out to be a lie. Only when the general
had confirmed it would they allow the bodies to be taken.
There were not enough men to dig so many graves, so the
wives of the dead men helped. I stood there with Mr. Wolf's
children watching their mother fill the grave. All the children
from Wisznica whose fathers had been shot were at the cemetery. Many of the children had chocolate in their hands,
which the soldiers had given them. People said it was the
Austrians, because they did not beat Jews but only took the
merchandise from their stores. They summoned the boys
who spoke Yiddish and talked with them, laughing. At the
cemetery I saw children throwing that chocolate away. I
returned to Bielsko with Mrs. Wolf, her sister-in-law, and
Masha, whose husband had also been killed in Wisznica. We
were joined by a boy who did not look Jewish and who spoke
good German. He would stop German soldiers and get bread
and canned goods, which he would share with us. Once a
German patrol asked him who we were. He said we were
orphans whose fathers had been killed. The Germans asked,
"Who killed them?" "Bandits," the boy replied.

The Germans entered Goworowo on September 6. The
next day, for no reason, they shot at doors and windows and
burned down the synagogue. All men between the ages of

seventeen and forty were rounded up and sent to Prussia to work. They didn't bother searching for people in hiding; they simply set fire to the houses. One hundred fifty people died at that time. My father and older brother were hiding in the cellar. When we ran out of food, we crept out at night and walked in the direction of the River Bug.

The Germans entered Brok before evening and ordered all the Jews to assemble in the church. The old Jews took the Torah scrolls with them. The Germans shut the church and announced that they would burn it down with us inside. The crying and wailing went on all night. The next day the younger men were taken away for labor and the rest were let go. Many Jews whose houses had been burned down came to us. German soldiers kept coming in, and they would take things or destroy them. Once they came for a few kilograms of flour and dumped the whole sack. Then that night they set fire to our house; we barely managed to escape. After that fire, only one Jewish house was left standing, the *shoykhet* Shmul's, and everyone took refuge there. In the night, the Germans knocked at the door. We could not open it immediately because of all the people sleeping on the floor. When we opened it, they shot the first Jew they saw. His name was Kaprański. They searched the house, taking everything of any value, then marched all the men, including my father, to the marketplace and shot them. Only the *shoykhet* and the rabbi managed to hide and slip out of the town by night, but on the way to Ostrów they encountered a German car. Two Germans got out and shot the *shoykhet*. The rabbi they wounded and left there on the road. He dragged himself to Ostrów and from there managed to get to Vilna. A peasant we knew ferried my mother and me to the other side of the river, and we stayed for a while with Szczeciner, the Jewish squire. When we learned that the Bolsheviks had taken Brok, we went back to the town. But four days later the Bolsheviks announced that they were leaving, so we drove by cart to Kossów, where my married brother lived.

When the Germans entered Włodawa, the Jews hid in cellars and attics, because the Germans were taking people for labor and then beating them to death. We were shaking with fear, but we were not allowed to cry, because the Germans might hear us. After a few days the Germans dragged the men, including our father, out of hiding and shut them in the synagogue. They would not let the women come close, and said they would burn the synagogue down. The women stood there until evening. Then they had to leave because Jews were not allowed on the streets after dark. We did not sleep a wink that night. Mama stood by the window and looked out toward the synagogue. When dawn came, she took a basket of food and went to the synagogue with a number of other women. At noon everyone was released and the Germans left Włodawa, then the Russians occupied the town. Eight days later, when we heard that the Russians were leaving, all the Jews packed up their bundles and moved to Włodawka on the other side of the Bug.

We fled Różan and went to Włodawa. But when the Germans arrived and the persecution of the Jews began, we moved to Ostrów Mazowiecka, where our cousin lived. In Ostrów the Germans made pogroms against the Jews, and the Poles helped them. Many Jews fled to the Soviet side. Those who stayed behind were older people, the sick, and families with small children.

The Germans stopped us near Ostrów and took my eighteen-year-old brother Chaim to Komorowo, where the Polish barracks were. For three days and three nights they were ordered to kneel in the mud with no food or water. At night searchlights were beamed onto them, and anyone who moved was machine-gunned. Two Polish prisoners of war near Chaim were hit by bullets, and many people died of exhaustion. Then they were ordered to pave the road. Only on the fifth day were they given a piece of bread and parcels from their families. When my brother came back three weeks later we could hardly recognize him.

The Germans occupied Wyszków on September 9; for a whole week they did the rounds of Jewish apartments, stealing what they could. On Saturday they ordered all the Jews out into the field. I hid in the cellar. I heard my brothers crying and my mother begging them to leave us alone: we were poor people, they could get nothing from us. I lay in the cellar for two days and two nights. I was afraid to leave even to get a drop of water. I could feel my strength fading and I asked God to call me to Him, because I was sure that none of my family would come back. On Monday the Germans searched the whole house and dragged me out. They tossed me onto the ground like a sack and kicked me with their heavy boots. I did not cry out or moan: I was incapable of making a sound. They dragged me out onto the street, where there stood five hundred other Jews who had been found hiding. A couple of men supported me under my arms. The Germans marched us out into a field and ordered us to stand there for several hours. Those men kept me propped up, because we had been threatened that anyone who sat down would be shot. Suddenly a truck with a machine gun drove up and people were mowed down. I fell along with the others. I did not know whether I was dead or alive. It was completely dark when I felt a kick in my side. I was terrified that it was the corpses rising from the dead. After the second kick I turned my head and saw Mr. Stański. He helped me up and dragged me to the forest. He told me that as soon as he'd heard the shots he'd dropped to the ground and pretended to be dead. He had checked to see if anyone else was alive, but no one had moved apart from me. The night was so dark we could not see each other, and I lost Mr. Stański in the forest. I was afraid to call out to him in case the Germans heard. I lay down and fell asleep. The next morning, I walked to a village, but the first people I saw there were Germans with a huge dog. They sicced it on me and laughed when it bit me in the leg. I stanched the bleeding with mud and dragged myself to Wilko, where several Jewish families lived. They took me in, dressed my wound, and gave me something to eat. I watched their cows for them, but my heart was uneasy, and after three days I went looking for my family. The bridge had been destroyed, and a woman ferried me across the river in a boat. I spent the night at her place. The next day, as I walked toward Wyszków, I saw my mother and both of my brothers on the road. They told me how the Germans had held them in the field and ordered them to kneel all day and all night. The children cried, the old people fainted, the women were in despair at their families' suffering. The Germans did not even let them relieve themselves, and talked loudly among themselves about the death trucks that would be arriving to kill them all like dogs. In the morning they were ordered to fall into line. They could not straighten themselves up and were beaten over the head with the butts of rifles. They were then told to run. Anyone who ran too slowly they shot. Again the next night they were ordered to kneel, and then made to run; and so on for four days. On the fifth day the men were loaded onto trucks and the women and children were released. My mother and brothers returned to Wyszków, but the house had been robbed bare, so they were walking toward Pułtusk in order to get to the Russian side.

When we heard that the Germans were nearing Pułtusk, we decided to escape to Wyszków. But the town was in flames and we had to keep going. German planes were firing at us, so we hid in the forest by day and walked at night. We reached Węgrów, and my father rented an apartment, which we shared with my uncle and aunt and their son, who were escaping with us. On the very day the Germans took Węgrów, my stepmother gave birth to a baby girl. My father had to hide because the Germans were rounding up Jews for labor. They beat them and cut off their beards—along with pieces of their faces. One day they came to our house. My father hid in the bed and I covered him up carefully. They searched everywhere but didn't come near the bed, because on it lay my stepmother, fresh from childbirth and white with horror. When they left, we called the doctor, who told us that if he had come five minutes later he would not have been able to save her. On Yom Kippur the Germans shot the rabbi because the Jews refused to work on the holiday. They arrived while he was leading the prayers and shot him on the spot. Everyone in town cried. After that my uncle took his family back to Przasnysz, but they were not allowed in and returned to us. Things got worse and worse in Węgrów. The

Germans were taking people away, and they never came back again. My father was afraid to leave the house and was not earning anything. We were afraid we would have nothing to live on, so when the baby was a month old my stepmother picked her up, and my father, my little brother, and I hoisted our bundles onto our backs and walked to the Russian border.

In Pułtusk the Jews were afraid to go outside because the Germans were beating and killing people and tearing out their beards. My sister was also afraid, because they would order girls to strip off their clothes and scrub the floors with their underwear.

They went from house to house beating people, taking money, and seizing people for labor. Many apartments and stores were robbed of everything.

An officer and two other Germans came to my father's workshop and demanded that he make them three pairs of boots—in a single night. When my father explained that it was impossible, they threatened to shoot him like a dog if the boots were not ready. My father worked all night with his journeymen. The next morning the Germans came, put on the boots, and paid not a penny for them. From then on they kept coming all the time, ordering boots without paying. Once a very fat officer came and took my father with him to measure other officers for boots.

The Germans visited a saddler we knew and took all his cord; they ordered me to carry it to the bridge for securing the girders, since they were swaying after the bombing. I saw Jews and Poles lined up by the river. The Germans were shooting at them, and they were falling into the water. I ran home half-dead with fear.

Two weeks after war broke out, the Germans entered Pułtusk and immediately began to persecute the Jews. Many were taken to the camps, and fifty Jews were burned behind the bridge. They ordered them to douse one another with gasoline, then set fire to them. Among them was my uncle Itzhak, along with his wife and five children.

The Germans entered Siedlce on September 11, and by the

third day had started to persecute the Jews. They dragged all
the men out of their homes and put them in jail. They kept
them there for forty-eight hours without food or drink, two
or three hundred of them in a single cell. They ripped the
clothes off them and beat them. After a few days the order
came for all the men to assemble in the town square; they
would shoot anyone they found at home. The men were
marched to Węgrów. My father was an elderly man with a
bad heart. He knew that he would never make it to Węgrów,
and that what he faced was death from a German bullet somewhere outside town, where he would not even be buried. On
the other hand, if they killed him in Siedlce maybe he could
count on the Jews to arrange a decent burial for him. So when
they were walking down a narrow street, my father ran into
the doorway of one of the houses. A German shot at him, but
missed. On Yom Kippur the few men who had managed to
stay in town prayed in our house.

When the Germans entered Siedlce, we hid in the garden.
A German came into the yard and asked our neighbor if she
was Jewish. She said she was not. The Germans could not tell
the difference, but Polish boys and women would follow
them around and point out the Jewish stores. In return for
this they were allowed to take whatever they wanted. The
Germans took only chocolate, but the Poles would cart away
shoes, clothes, fabric—whole loads of stuff. Even eighty-
year-old Jews were taken away for labor. When they had no
work for them, they made them stand for hours on end with
their hands held high, and they photographed them. My
father was taken to the labor camp at Węgrów. When we
learned that the German overseer there took bribes, my sister
Rachela and I went and bought our father's freedom for ten
złotys. His beard had been torn out and he looked like death.
Once my mother sent me to the *beys medresh* with a bowl of
food for a lunatic she looked after. When I got there I saw
Germans tossing out the Holy Books and trampling on them.
I ran back home in terror. Jews who had been driven out of
other towns were put into the *beys medresh*. They begged in
the streets and sang in the courtyards. Most of them were

from Kalisz. They ate in a kitchen set up for them by the Jewish community. One day we learned that the Germans were leaving and the Bolsheviks were coming. There was great joy in the town that morning when we saw the big Russian tanks. The Jews opened their stores and sold what they could—there was not much left after the German looting. In our store, we had only cigarettes and a couple of barrels of herring. The Russian soldiers had piles of Polish money. They did not haggle and bought everything we had. When we heard that the Russians were to leave Siedlce and that anyone who wanted to could go with them, my oldest brother took the four youngest of us along with him, while the older children remained with my father. Freight cars crammed with civilians were hitched onto the military train.

When the Germans entered Długosiodło, they shot the first Jew they saw on the street. I do not remember his name, but he was the brother-in-law of our friend Paskowicz. Soon thousands of Jews who had been driven out of Wyszków arrived, nearly naked and barefoot. Poor, tiny Długosiodło had no room for so many people. A communal kitchen was set up, but money was lacking for everything.

When we got to Długosiodło the town was overflowing with refugees, and we spent the night in a stable. On the third day the Germans threw us out of Długosiodło, and when we started on our way they began to shoot. They ran after us, and grabbed the men and cut off their beards. The next day we arrived in Ostrołęka and met our aunt there. She had been the last to leave Pułtusk, and she told us the names of people the Germans had shot. We cried a lot, because some of our relatives were among them.

As soon as the Germans entered Kałuszyn, they ordered all Poles and all Jews to assemble in the church. We saw a German grab our rabbi, Naftali, by the beard and shove him into the church. In the church they told us to stand with our hands up. They searched everyone and took everything of any value. After the search they beat us. Later the mayor, a Pole, arrived; he got permission from the Germans to let the women and children go home. Then the Poles were released, but the Jewish men were taken away for labor. My father's job was burying the dead. They loaded the corpses onto carts, which they had to pull themselves. The Germans goaded them on with their riding crops to make them run faster. They beat Jews on the streets and tore out their beards. One older German was kind: he came to our neighbor, who was a shoemaker, and paid him for repairing his boots.

The Germans took Łańcut eight days after war broke out. They went from house to house, beating, tearing out beards, taking people away for labor—many never came back. They looted all the valuables, and the local people followed every step of the way, waiting for anything the Germans would let them have.

In Łańcut the Germans beat the Jews and robbed the Jewish homes and market stalls. Anything they did not want they passed out to the local people, who willingly helped them with their robbery.

Three days before Rosh Hashana, the Germans entered Leżajsk and began their activities by tormenting the Jews. They rounded them up for labor, beat them, tore out their beards with shreds of flesh attached, and set fire to the *beys medresh*. They wanted to burn down the synagogue too, but it stood between Christian houses and they were afraid the fire would spread. The Jews had to clean the barracks and wash the tanks; the German overseers didn't think twice about using their riding crops.

The Germans entered Leżajsk two days before Rosh Hashana. People were afraid to go to services because the Germans had picked up one old Jew on his way to the synagogue and cut off his beard—along with part of his face. On the second day of Rosh Hashana, the Germans set fire to the synagogue and the *talmud-torah;** they stood there to make sure no one tried to put it out. In exchange for a large sum of

*Children's religious school.

money, they gave us permission to save the Torah. On Yom Kippur, services were held in our basement. The children stood outside to see if anyone was coming.

The Germans took Niemirów on September 12. The next day a crowd of Ukrainian peasants arrived in carts, men and women with sacks, and set about looting the Jewish stores. A delegation from the community went to see the Germans to ask for protection. The commandant, who turned out to be an Austrian, sent out patrols to chase the robbers away. The Austrians warned us that the SS would soon be coming and things would be bad for us then. On Sunday, September 17, the real Germans came, and they started to beat the Jews. By Yom Kippur no one was allowed to say prayers, and a group of Jews, including my father, held secret prayers in the attic while we lads stood guard. The next day an officer we had become friendly with, a Viennese, came and said he was bringing good news: the Bolsheviks were coming.

On the first day after Mieliec was taken, no one was bothered. So the *shoykhets* Chaim and Yasha, and Yasha's son-in-law, went to slaughter a few head of cattle for the holidays. Suddenly some Germans burst in, shouting, "There they are, the Jewish murderers!" and they shot all three of them. Then they went to the *mikva*,* which was full of people because it was the day before the holidays. They herded everyone naked to the slaughterhouse, where they shot sixty-four Jews. A few days later they set fire to the synagogue, the *beys medresh*, and the house where Rabbi Hurwicz lived with his twelve-year-old ward, an orphan boy. The rabbi jumped out the window and was saved. But the boy got stuck on a fence as he tried to escape, and a German killed him.

The Germans entered Nachal during Rosh Hashana and handed out cigarettes on the street. Five days later the Poles retook the town by storm. The next day the Germans returned and set fire to the town, as punishment. Nachman the cattle trader ran to save his animals and was shot. Leibish Zalkind wanted to save the Torah from the synagogue. The

---

*Ritual bathhouse.

Germans locked him in the synagogue together with a few other Jews and burned them, together with the scrolls.

The Germans entered Tomaszów when we were in the synagogue. Everyone was frightened but finished their prayers before rushing home. The following day the Germans set fire to the *beys medresh* and the synagogue. The Jews were afraid to leave their houses, because every day there were roundups in the streets. Jewish men had their beards cut off and were forced to do the filthiest kinds of work, from which some never came back. My father hid in the attic. The Germans robbed the Jewish stores. They kept the more valuable things for themselves and gave the cheaper stuff to the crowd of youngsters that followed them around. Then the Germans left the town and for two days no one was in charge. On the first day of Sukkos[*] the Russian tanks arrived; the Jews came out of their hiding places and breathed freely. The Russians bought everything that had not been looted. We thought they would stay until the end of the war. When we found out eight days later that they were leaving and that the Germans were coming back for good, we did not want to believe it. Many Jews left Tomaszów, including our family.

The Germans entered Tomaszów Lubelski during Rosh Hashana. The very first day they killed Rabbi Nachum, Rafał Bernsztajn, and a boy called Lipe. Many people who were taken away for labor never came back, including Rabbi Isar, the head of the yeshiva. The Germans' first visit to our town was a brief one, but they managed to loot all the Jewish stores and houses and call out the Poles to pick up the leftovers. Then the Russians came and, like a ravening horde, pounced on whatever we had managed to hide from the Germans. At first they paid, but later they stole too. When they announced that they were not going to stay in Tomaszów and that any- one who wanted could leave with them, my father decided we would go to Choroszów, where my grandmother and my uncle lived.

[*]The Feast of Tabernacles.

The Germans entered Przeworsk during Rosh Hashana, and the first thing they did was to set fire to the big synagogue. Three times they doused the building with gasoline and three times the fire went out. They became furious and grabbed the holy scrolls out of the ark and trampled on them. When the building was finally in flames they took photographs of it. A number of houses on Kazimierzowska Street burned down too, but the *beys medresh* next to the synagogue miraculously escaped because the wind was blowing in the opposite direction. Two days after Yom Kippur, the Germans ordered all Jewish men, on pain of death, to assemble in the courtyard of the convent. My father and my twenty-year-old brother Efraim went. They were expecting the worst, but Rabbi Frenkel comforted people, telling them the Holy Books prophesied that the Messiah would be coming soon. They were then told to line up, and the German commandant shouted, "Where is the rabbi?" The rabbi was in hiding. The Germans threatened to kill several Jews if he did not appear. When the rabbi came, the Germans went crazy. They tore out his beard and beat him unconscious. Then they flogged everyone and ordered them to crawl on all fours. They called this "calisthenics for the Jews." Most of all they beat the old men who were not up to the exercises. When the Germans had beaten everyone bloody, they went up and down the rows, holding out their helmets and ordering everyone to throw in their money, watches, and fountain pens.

In Przeworsk the Germans desecrated the cemetery and took the gravestones to pave the streets. They set fire to the synagogue and the *beys medresh;* they did not allow anyone to put out the fire or save the Holy Books. When the rabbi ran in to save the Torah, the Germans caught him and, as punishment, levied a high tribute on the town. The Jews of Przeworsk could not come up with so much money, but the Lwów community came to their aid.

On September 13, during Rosh Hashana, the Germans took Lesko. A few days later they levied a very high tribute on the Jewish population. The Jews in our town were poor, and we had no choice but to flee to Sokal, which was on the boundary of the two occupations: the train station was occupied by the Germans and the rest by the Russians. We left all of our belongings with a Ukrainian peasant, and he drove us to the River San. The border was not well guarded and we easily reached the other side.

After the Germans entered Lesko, they accused the Jews of pouring hot water over the German soldiers and imposed a levy of one million złotys on the town. They arrested twenty-four people as hostages; they grabbed Jews for labor, even though the community said it would undertake to provide the manpower. I saw Jewish men having their beards ripped out. It was difficult to collect the million złotys. Among those who contributed were a few elderly Poles. The tribute money was paid, but the Germans did not release their hostages and announced that they would hold them until the Jews handed over their hidden merchandise. They looted the stores every day. When they had taken all our goods, my mother and I decided to make our way to Sokal, where my father was. At the border, the Germans stripped us naked and ripped up our clothes searching for diamonds. They kept us without food for twenty-four hours, then they made us drink castor oil to get the diamonds out of us. They beat us terribly. When we staggered across the border, the Russians took all the best things we had on us, and we arrived in Sokal half-naked.

My father was a wealthy, well-known man in our town and was afraid that the Germans would take him hostage. So he fled Jarosław together with my older brother Józef. They wandered through towns and villages for two weeks, then came home saying that the whole of Poland was occupied and there was nowhere to escape to, and if you had to die, then better to die at home.

In Jarosław the Germans and the Ukrainians robbed the Jews of everything they could. If they could not take something with them, they destroyed it. They grabbed people on the street. My father was ordered to clean toilets with his bare hands.

The Germans entered Rozwadów on the second day of Rosh Hashana and ordered that all the stores be opened, on pain of death. When the stores were open, they set about looting them. Some officers came to Zysel Zylber and took away all his clothes. A German came to us carrying a revolver and demanded our linens. My father said he could have them even without the revolver.

In Rozwadów Jews were ordered to take off their shirts, wash the floors and windows of German apartments with them, and then put them back on again. They cut off the rabbi's beard and ordered him to clean the toilet with his bare hands. Germans and Poles looked on, and they all laughed out loud.

On our way to the holiday services, we heard rumors that the Germans were coming, so my father harnessed the horse and we fled Dubienka. We said prayers in a barn we came across. The rabbi, who was traveling with us, had a shofar* with him, so the service took place according to the rules. We spent the whole day in the barn, then traveled all night; we did the same the next day and night. My father drove the weary horse hard, for fear that the Germans would catch up with us. So we arrived at Kamień Kaszyrski. We could not get a place to stay because of the flood of refugees, so we moved into the *beys medresh*.

On September 14, the Germans entered Łaszczów with tanks, bringing Polish prisoners of war with them. My father leaned out the window to see where they were taking them, and a German soldier took aim at him. But my father managed to duck. Then several Germans burst into our store and began looting, shouting that they were going to shoot us. The next day, the Germans fled because there was a battle in the nearby Tomaszów forest, which the Poles managed to win. A few tanks were left behind in the town, as well as dead German soldiers in the streets. The retreating Polish army had burned down the warehouses, later on the Germans set fire to anything they could, so many houses were burned down, including ours, but we were overjoyed at the Germans'

---

*Ram's horn, blown on the High Holidays.

defeat. Two days before Yom Kippur the Germans took the town again, but every last one of them was killed by Polish soldiers who came in from the Tomaszów forest. Again we were very pleased, but on Yom Kippur the Germans came back with a huge force of tanks and guns, bringing with them large groups of prisoners of war. We realized that the Poles were no longer offering any resistance. The next day the Germans withdrew and the Russians moved in, in their place, but a month later the town was given back to the Germans.

The Germans entered from one end of Biłgoraj, while Poles were hiding in the woods at the other end. The shooting went on all Saturday night and Sunday, but by Monday the Germans had started to run the place. When they saw a bearded Jew they would set fire to his beard, tear his cap off his head, and beat him. They ordered Jews to sing and dance, and to beat and insult each other. Young Polish boys would run with the Germans and point out the Jewish houses to them. Then they would go in and take what they wanted. After the holidays the Germans left Biłgoraj, and for four days the town fell prey to outlaws. When the Russians came, a citizens' militia composed of Jews and Christians was organized. The Bolsheviks were in Biłgoraj for just eight days, and yet they bought up all the food in town. They stuffed their coat pockets with big packages of herring, which they had apparently not eaten in a long time. But they did no one any harm and were happy to talk with anyone on the street. When they left, the militia continued to maintain order until the subsequent arrival of the Germans. At first the Germans pretended not to see us, but a few days later the Gestapo arrived, and they went through apartments, robbing them, beating people for no reason, and threatening that the worst was yet to come. At six in the morning they began firing at the windows, and when we ran out of our houses they grabbed the men and forced them to crush stones on the road. They kept them there until ten in the evening, but Jews were only allowed outside until seven, so they stayed in the ditches until morning. My father was taken to a big square, where he collected garbage all day. When it got dark and he said he wanted to go home, they beat him so badly that he moaned all night from the pain. We could see that he would not last long like this, so we decided to flee to the Russians.

In Limanowa the Germans arrested the wealthiest Jews and were searching for my father. Several times they took hostages to a field, ordered them to dig graves, then brought them back to jail. One day they ordered the entire Jewish population to assemble in the market square, on pain of death. When we were all assembled, a drunken Gestapo commandant announced that seventeen hostages had been sentenced to death, and we were all herded off to the cemetery. Some consoled themselves that this time too it was just to scare us. The Germans ordered the hostages to dig graves and did not allow anyone to help them. When the graves were ready, the Germans opened fire with machine guns. After these experiences, I escaped to my father in Tarnów. In Tarnów the Germans came to our house and took my father to the barber's. There they tied his hands and one of them began to chop off his beard with a blunt bayonet, wounding his face in the process. I went down on my knees in front of them and kissed their hands, but the more I begged the more they tortured him. I took my unconscious father home, and he stayed in bed for weeks. I witnessed many such beard-cutting scenes. I also saw the Germans herding Jews into the new synagogue and firing cannons at the building while the dying cried, "*Shma Yisroel.*"[*]

The Germans took Przemyśl on September 14. The next day they arrested Mr. Herszfeld, with whom I was staying. A few days later he came home all beaten up. He was in pain for two weeks before he died. In the same house lived a doctor, who had not returned home for a long time. His family later recognized him among the dead by the thermometer in his pocket. The Germans remained in Przemyśl for a few weeks. As they left town they demolished many houses and blew up the *beys medresh*. I saw Jews and Poles working to put out

---

[*] "Hear, O Israel, the Lord is our God, the Lord is One," a prayer that is part of the daily liturgy and that is spoken by Jews on the point of death.

the fire. Generally speaking, Jews and Poles helped each other out.

In Przemyśl the Germans carried out a roundup on Franciszkańska Street, and they shot six hundred Jews they caught in the woods outside town. When the Russians arrived, the Jewish community convinced them to let them dig up their dead and rebury them in the Jewish cemetery. People identified family members by their clothes and by what they had in their pockets. They were buried in a place of honor, each in a separate grave. Only those who could not be identified were placed in a common grave. From the inscriptions on the graves I remembered Dr. Tirkel, a well-known surgeon who had operated on my older brother. They said that the director of the Jewish hospital was also among the dead.

On Saturday evening, German tanks marked with swastikas rolled into Krasnobród. The Germans handed out chocolate and white bread to the children, talked with the Jews, and did not beat anyone. The next day the tanks left and the *real* Germans arrived; they immediately started on the Jews. People praying at the *beys medresh* were chased out and ordered to bury dead horses wrapped in *taleysim*.* Then they began to loot Jewish stores. The Poles pointed out which ones were owned by Jews. The worst came on Thursday, on the first day of Sukkos, when the Germans were to hand the town over to the Bolsheviks. They poured gasoline over the houses, set fire to them, and did not let people escape. They burned down a beautiful synagogue that had just been built shortly before the war. One old Jew ran up and asked to be allowed to save the Torah. They said they would let him if he unrolled it on the ground and danced on it. I don't know how many Jews perished in the flames, but I do know that Cantor Shmul Eliezer and his son burned to death. On Friday, when the Bolsheviks arrived, the Jews took sheets and gathered up the charred remains in order to give them a ritual burial. The Russians stayed in the town for only two days. When the

---

*Prayer shawls.

commander announced that the border was being pushed back seventy kilometers and that anyone who wanted could go with them, we all left with the Russians.

In Chełm the Germans herded several hundred Jews outside town and ordered them to dig their own graves. Among the dead were the town's most prominent people, including some good friends of ours. My mother was out of her mind with despair.

In Krzeszów the Germans killed many of our friends, including Manes Zyndel the glazier. They caught Moishe Bursztajn and the rabbi's son, and ordered them to dig their own graves. They shot Bursztajn but said it would be a waste of a bullet on the other one because he might be useful as a laborer. They also killed a number of Jewish women. They pulled off Roza Bokser's ring, together with her finger, before murdering her. That was two days before the Russians arrived.

As soon as they entered Zagórze, the Germans beat the Jews, tore out their beards, and ordered them to dance in the marketplace. My father did not come out of hiding. Since our tavern was known for its good wines and liquors, some of the officers came to my father and assured him that if he opened the tavern he would come to no harm. Other places they looted and kicked out the owners, but they really did nothing to my father. Some paid for their vodka, some didn't. My father was pleased not to be harassed and never demanded money. Every night the Germans surrounded a number of houses and hounded Jewish families out of town without letting them take anything with them. We could hear the crying and the wailing.

When they arrived in Osiany Dolne, the Germans forced the Jews to perform difficult and humiliating tasks. They beat them and ordered them to cut each other's beards off, and they ordered the women to wash floors with their own underwear.

When the Germans appeared in Majdan, we hid with a peasant my father used to buy cattle from. We sat in the stable and did not go outside, so that the neighbors would not see us. Then the peasant told us he was afraid to keep us any longer, so we left by night and went back home. We found our door open and the house looted. A few days later, the Germans surrounded the Jewish quarter and herded all the men to the marketplace. There they gave them cans of gasoline and ordered them to pour it over the synagogue. When the synagogue was in flames, they forced the Jews to dance around it while they split their sides laughing. We could not stand this, and we managed with the help of some smugglers to make our way to Niemirów, on the Russian side.

Immediately after the Germans arrived in Majdan, trucks pulled up to our house and drove away with the entire contents of our stockrooms. The same thing happened to other Jewish storekeepers. The Germans kept the most valuable things for themselves and gave the rest to the Christians; so in just a few hours the Jews were robbed of everything they had. The Germans viciously tortured the Jews, put them to forced labor, and herded them out of the town—they never returned.

On the Sunday after Yom Kippur, the Germans entered Biała Góra and started looting Jewish property, eagerly assisted by the local people. We decided to return to Wieliczka: if we had to live under German occupation, better to be at home. In Leżajsk we were stopped by German guards, who would not let Jews onto the bridge. A few Poles were having a friendly chat with the guards, identifying whom to let through and whom to stop. We waited until evening and hired a boat. We did not recognize our town, it was so ruined. When we learned that the Germans had murdered five of our relatives, along with many other Jews, we got back into our cart and drove to Sienawa. There were no Germans or Russians there yet, but the citizens' militia, made up of both Christians and Jews, did not allow refugees to stay in the town for fear of starvation and threatened tough penalties for harboring people. We went to stay with a peasant outside town. The situation improved once the Bolsheviks arrived.

The Germans burned down all the synagogues in Bielsko and Biała. Every day they came looking for our father. They searched the closets and under the beds; they turned the whole apartment upside down. They transported many of the Jews they caught to a place called the Gypsy forest. People said they mistreated them terribly there and killed them. When the order came for all Jews to be deported from Bielsko, my mother bought a train ticket to Kielce, but we went all the way to Łódź, where her brother lived and where one of our distant relatives was a baker. My mother would pick up baked goods from him and sell them on the street, but she was afraid to stay in Łódź because Jews were being beaten up in the streets. We took the train to Warsaw, and my mother gave all the money we had in exchange for space in a truck that took us to the Russian border.

There were many Germans living in our neighborhood, and we had friendly relations with them. But on the very day that the German army entered Łódź, they stopped recognizing us on the street. When my father arrived at the factory, the foreman, who was a German, wouldn't let him in. They searched our apartment, then the foreman came with a Gestapo man and demanded the keys to the warehouse, so we were left with nothing. One day fourteen Jews were dragged out of a café on Piotrkowska Street and shot on the highway. Among them were Bister and Szafir, factory owners and friends of my father's. After this, we got on a train and went to Małkinia. At the station we had to pass between rows of Germans beating Jews over the head and taking their money and valuables. Then we waited for two days in no-man's-land.

When the Germans occupied Warsaw, they began to distribute bread, but Jews were thrown off the lines.

When the news reached us that the Germans were giving out soup and bread, my mother, who did not look Jewish, would go out and bring back something for us to eat. After a while people found out she was Jewish. She was thrown off the line and returned home beaten bloody. When my father saw that she had been beaten, he said he wouldn't stay in Warsaw another minute. We packed our bundles and went to Małkinia. The Germans were beating Jews and taking their property in Małkinia, but a Pole who had been traveling in the same train compartment as us claimed that we were his family, so we escaped a beating. The border was always opened for just a few minutes, so people stayed awake at night. We were hungry, and we had to walk a long way to get water. It was raining and the fire refused to light. When the border was suddenly opened in the middle of the night, everyone rushed across, trampling each other. Everyone was shouting and calling out, and lost children cried in the dark. My mother tied us to her with a piece of string, and that was how we ran across to the other side.

As a carpenter, my father had a lot of work in Warsaw, because after the bombing people needed their windows and doors repaired. We would have had enough to live on if it hadn't been for the Germans' constantly taking my father away for labor, after which he would come home beaten. One day when he came back he said he wasn't staying in Warsaw one day longer, and the next morning we took a cab to the Eastern Station, where we found thousands of refugees. In Małkinia my mother and I stood among the Christians, and that is how we got through. But then we could not find my father. We were kept in the neutral zone for two days; it was pouring and we were swamped in mud. Finally the border was opened and we made it over to the other side, along with a crowd of other people. We walked as far as Zaręby and then took the train to Białystok. My father was waiting for us at the station.

Immediately after they entered Warsaw, the Germans began snatching Jews to clean the town. They beat them and tore out their beards, and looted Jewish apartments. They took the felt from my father's hat shop and said they were going to send it to their wives. We packed a few things and went to Małkinia. At the station, all the men were taken away. The women refused to budge without their husbands. The Germans threatened to shoot. We pulled back, but only a short way, and I could see my father and the other Jewish men being taken to a building from where we later heard screaming. We children started to cry. My father came back covered with blood, then we went into the border zone. When on the third day they opened the border, we ran for it like crazy, even though the Russians were firing to scare us off.

When the bombing stopped, my father went to his store. The Germans stopped him outside, cut off half his beard, bloodied his face, and took his merchandise. My mother was crying, and the neighbors rushed in to have a look at my father. Some advised him to shave off the rest of his beard; others said he should walk around the way he was. My father did not shave it, and the Germans stopped him again and beat him for not having shaved off the other half of his beard. My mother began sobbing uncontrollably, so my father shaved his beard and went into town to get some money so that we could leave. But he did not come back that night. The next day some Polish friends told us that the Germans had taken him and some other Jews to clean the Parliament building. Four days later my father returned with swollen hands. He said he would rather die of hunger than leave the house again. My mother herself went to our debtors to collect money for our journey to Russia.

For three days and three nights we waited by the River Bug because it was a full moon and no one wanted to take us across. We hid in peasant huts. German soldiers would come by to have some fun with the Polish girls, and while they were at it they would catch the Jews and demand ransom money from them. They would hunt down Jews who wanted to get to the other side and would beat and rob those that they caught. When there was finally a moonless night, my father tore open his lining, removed two hundred złotys, and gave them to a peasant, who ferried us across. The commander of the German guards took that money from him in our presence. In the middle of the river, we collided in the dark with another boat, which capsized, and two children drowned.

The Germans came to the peasant's house where we were staying and beat my mother with a riding crop. They also beat us young children. Then our father returned from Brest and picked us up in a car. The Germans stopped us on the way and beat us. But we made it to the Bug and reached the other side in a little boat.

At midnight on Yom Kippur, a truck full of storm troopers arrived in the marketplace. They gave orders for all Jews to leave Długosiodło and go to their "friends on the other side." Everyone packed in a hurry and the storm troopers tore through the houses stealing whatever took their fancy. At two in the morning we heard shots, so we ran out of the house. The storm troopers were chasing everyone out onto the road to Zambrów. The road went through a forest, and we stopped to catch our breath. Since it was Yom Kippur, my father and other observant Jews said a prayer, then sang a religious melody and danced.

Before Sukkos my mother went to the *shoykhet* to have him slaughter a goose. Suddenly my father came rushing in and said the Germans had chased him out of his workshop and taken his keys away. Even before he had finished speaking, my mother ran in with the news that the Germans were expelling all the Jews from Pułtusk. We helped our parents pack whatever came to hand. Each of us took a bundle, and we walked across the bridge, where tanks were stationed. The Germans were prodding the Jews on; anyone walking too slowly was thrown into the water. We stopped in the village of Popławiec, where my mother's aunt lived. The next day the Germans came looking for my father. They said that he would come to no harm and that he should go back to his workshop. But my father stayed hidden, and when the Germans left we continued on our way. Outside Pułtusk we saw people on fire. They were Jews from Wyszków who had wanted to come to the aid of the Jews who had been driven out of Pułtusk. The Germans captured them and doused them with gasoline. We walked to the station, where there was a train leaving for Białystok.

During Sukkos, the Germans came to my grandfather's warehouse while my father was there. The neighbors saw the

Germans take my father out into the yard, beat him, take his money, tear up his papers, and hound him to who-knows-where. That same day all the Jews were ordered to leave Pułtusk. A Christian we knew gave us a cart to get to Popławiec. On the bridge the Germans ordered all the adults to get out of the cart. They shot people and threw them into the water. We cried bitterly, for we were afraid of being left alone. But my mother made it across the bridge and ran down the back roads because people were being killed on the main road. She found us again in Popławiec. My mother had no money left to hire a cart, so we continued on foot with our bundles over our shoulders. The peasants did not want to take us in for the night, but a couple of times we managed to spend the night in a barn. My mother bartered underwear for bread. After four days we reached Węgrów, where our relatives lived. To our great joy, we found my father and grandfather there. There were Russians in Węgrów at that time.

The Germans issued the order for all the Jews to be in the marketplace within fifteen minutes. Anyone failing to come would be shot. We were very scared, and we snuggled up to our parents. The Germans, wielding riding crops, searched everyone, even the little children, and they took whatever they wanted. Then they photographed us and ordered us onto the bridge. But the road was so congested that it was hard to get through. Suddenly, the Germans started shooting, and a number of people fell down dead. Panic ensued, with people falling into the river and mothers losing their children. When we had pushed our way through to the other side, Germans were standing along the road driving us on. The peasants were afraid to let us in.

We were told to assemble in the marketplace, where all Jews were ordered to leave Pułtusk within a few hours. We put together some small bundles; each of us carried one on our shoulders, and we walked to the bridge. German tanks were there, and we had to push our way through them, with the Germans laughing and shoving us against the tanks with their rifle butts. The bridge was half-destroyed and people were afraid to use it. Suddenly the Germans began firing, and

panic broke out. People were falling into the water and
drowning; children were getting lost in the crowd. My father
threw his bundle away and took my little brother on one arm
and me on the other. My mother grabbed two of the older
children by the hand, and that is how we made it across. Once
we got across the bridge, we kept running. The peasants did
not even want to let us into their barns, and we spent the
nights in fields until we reached the station and boarded a
train for Białystok.

The Germans ordered all Jews to assemble in the park
within fifteen minutes. There they told us to hand over our
money and jewelry; they searched us. Then they led everyone
to the bridge, which was surrounded by tanks. Anyone who
couldn't push his way through was thrown into the water. I
remember the crying of the children and the wailing of the
grown-ups. My father, mother, and older sisters were holding
me and little Moishe so tightly that I screamed, "Mama,
you'll strangle me!" On the other side of the bridge, my
father showed us a place where fifty Jews had been burned,
including our uncle and his family. Even though the Germans
were shooting at us, my father and a few other Jews stopped
and said a prayer for the dead. When we would walk through
a village, people would take pity on us and would give us
bread and water. We arrived on foot in Ostrów and from
there rode by cart to Zambrów.

The Germans gathered us all together in the square and
ordered us to leave Ostrów within an hour. We wanted to go
get our things, but the square was surrounded by machine
guns. They herded us toward the border, and they ripped the
clothes on our backs before letting us cross to the other side.

When we heard that the Germans were planning to expel
the Jews from Ostrołęka, my father hired a cart to Dąbrowa.
The Germans searched us and took our money and valuables
before letting us through to the Soviet side. We took the train
to Białystok, where we found throngs of refugees.

When the Germans expelled the Jews from Długosiodło,
my family went to Dąbrowa, and from there to Białystok. I
was in Warsaw throughout this time because I had caught

pneumonia during the bombing, and it was only after Sukkos that I left for Maków, where we had relatives. I rode in a cart with seven other Jews. The Germans stopped us on the way and forced us into a manor, beating us all the way. There they ordered us to load sacks onto some trucks. There were a few hundred Jews working there. Everyone had to lift a full sack. Some who wanted to give the weaker ones a hand were shot. They released us in the evening, and we got onto one of the many carts driving to the Soviet border. The Germans stopped us several times more and took what they wanted. In one place they removed one Jew from each cart, then they led them into the forest and ordered the rest of us to keep going and not look back. I thought I would find the Bolsheviks in Maków, but the Germans were there too. Along with the local Jews I experienced beatings and labor roundups, from which many never came back. A month later my sister arrived and took me to Białystok.

A month after they arrived in Włodawa, the Germans ordered all the Jews to assemble outside the town, from where they would be taken to the Soviet border. My father was not in town at the time, so we hid in the cellar of an abandoned house to wait for him. When my father returned, we heard heavy shooting from where the others were assembled. Six hundred Jews were shot, and the place where they were buried was tarred over for a gas station. We crept away by night and fled in the direction of the Soviet border.

Suwałki was first occupied by the Russians. When after a week we heard that the Russians were pulling out, everyone was terribly afraid, and many Jews left with the Russians for Augustów. Polish thugs ran through the streets beating up Jews. The Germans arrived after Sukkos and shot our friend Lubliński in the street—his son was living in Palestine. They robbed the Jewish stores and market stalls. Polish plainclothes policemen went from house to house searching for hidden merchandise. All the Jewish men were rounded up for labor. My father wasn't earning anything now because he had to constantly work for the Germans; several times he was beaten up on the street for no reason. When we heard that the

Germans were going to expel the Jews from Suwałki, my father hired a cart and we drove in the direction of the Soviet border.

In Jarosław the Germans started chasing the Jews over to the Russian side even before Yom Kippur, threatening to shoot anyone who tried to come back. We hid, thinking that this would pass and that we would be able to stay in our home, but on September 27 the German commandant issued the order that all Jews had to go over to the Bolsheviks within four hours. When the Jews arrived at the bank of the San with their heavy boxes, the Germans and Ukrainians took most of their things and let them cross the river with small bundles only.

The bridge over the San was shuddering, and people were afraid to set foot on it. The Germans threw anyone who hesitated into the water.

Immediately after Sukkos we heard shots. We ran out and saw Germans chasing Jews from Chełm and Hrubieszów across the river. The Russians had orders not to let anyone through. We begged the Russian soldiers to let them through, and the Jews cried, "Long live Stalin!" but it was no use. Finally a doctor, a Pole who dealt with refugee affairs, went to the Bolshevik commander and prevailed on him to let the Jews cross the border. At the border itself, the Germans announced that only four hundred Jews could cross. Because there were four hundred and eight, they shot eight young boys before everyone's eyes.

You can imagine the scene in Sokal when the entire Jewish population of Jarosław suddenly arrived and when, the next day, we were told that another thousand or so Jews had arrived from Hrubieszów during the night, having been forced to make the journey on foot.

The Jews who reached the Russian side were in tatters and streaming with blood. They said that the Germans had robbed them of everything.

Two weeks after they entered Leżajsk, the Germans ordered all the Jews to move, within one day, to the other side of the border.

When the Jews were ordered to leave Leżajsk, the peasants did not want to hire out their carts. People were paying three thousand złotys for a cart; only the rich could afford it. Most people left with their bundles on their backs. We broke our journey in the village of Charłupka on the other side of the San. My mother and my elder sister slipped back home a couple of times and brought some of the things we had left behind.

A few weeks after they arrived in Przeworsk, the Germans ordered the Jews to leave the town within one hour—anyone who stayed would be shot. We grabbed anything that came to hand and ran to the San. The Germans had commandeered all the boats and were demanding four hundred złotys a head. Not many families had that kind of money. Some tried to swim across, but the Germans shot at them; many people drowned.

On September 26, an officer read out the order that all Jews were to move to the Russian side at nine o'clock the following morning. It is hard to describe the scene in Przeworsk that night: people rushing to pack and dashing around in search of carts. Some gave peasants a whole house's worth of furniture for a ride. The peasant who took our furniture did not show up, and we had to go on foot. People were leaving the town in tears. On the way, the Germans unhitched the horses, and everyone, even the sick, had to walk the fifteen kilometers to the river. No one had the strength to carry the heavy packs of bedding, so they left them on the road. My mother was pregnant and it was very difficult for her to walk, but by some miracle we saw a peasant with an empty cart and my father prevailed on him to take pity on my mother, otherwise she would have dropped on the road. The peasant took a few sick people too. At the border, a Russian soldier called out to my father in Yiddish, "Look! The Red Messiah has come!" On the other side it was easier to get a cart, and we reached Krakowiec by evening. The town had been burned down, but light was filtering through one window. My father knocked at the door. A Jewish man opened the door and offered him a holiday greeting. At that moment my father remembered that it was Sukkos.

Three weeks after they arrived in Rozwadów, the Germans issued the order that all Jews were to cross to the other side of the San within one hour. Several thousand people rushed, panic-stricken, to the river, carrying the sick and the old, losing small children. There were only two boats, each with room for twenty people, but a hundred Jews were crammed into each one, because the Germans were clubbing them with their rifle butts and threatening to kill anyone who stayed behind. Finally we managed to get a large boat for a lot of money. When everyone had reached the other side, the Germans opened fire. We ran to the village, but the peasants would not let us in, so we trudged exhausted through the fields. Finally we chipped in with another family and bought a horse and cart to continue our journey. Ukrainians attacked us by night: they beat us up and took our cart with all our belongings. We walked to Kołoszyce, where some good people gave us shelter for the night. The town was brimming with refugees. Many were spending the night in the street.

At seven in the morning, all the Jews were assembled in the marketplace in Rozwadów. They were permitted to take only what they could carry. Homes and stores were left unprotected, so their Christian neighbors took what was left. The Germans beat the Jews. The old and the sick were dragged out of their beds—they could hardly stand on their feet. Prodded with bayonets, we ran to the sound of the Germans yelling, "Off you go to your Red brothers!" Mothers flung down their bags to carry young children. I led my four-year-old sister Sarele by the hand. On the riverbank the Germans searched people, and whoever had a watch was forced to hand it over. We were taken by boat to the other side.

In Rozwadów the Jews were told to gather in the marketplace at eight in the morning. Once they were assembled, they were searched and beaten, their money and valuables were taken away, and they were herded over to the other side

of the San. We hid in the cellar, and two days later set off for
Lwów. We took back roads because the Germans were beating Jews on the main roads.

After a month, the Germans gathered all the Jews of Zagórze in the marketplace and chased them out of town, allowing them to take only small bundles. My father wanted to
come with us, but the Germans held him along with a number of tailors and shoemakers, saying that they would let
them leave later. We walked to Lesko, where our relatives
lived. My father wrote to us at first, but then his letters
stopped. I do not know what happened to him. Soon after
this, the Germans chased the Jews out of Lesko. On the
bridge, they searched everyone and took away their belongings. Some of the wagons were not allowed through. They
stopped the cart my mother was riding on, and it was only
the next day that she found her way to us. We cried when she
told us what the Germans had done to the Jews there.

In Tarnobrzeg the Jews were told to leave the town within
two hours. The sick and the old who could not move were
killed. One Jewish man, who was lame and could barely walk,
was killed by a German with an iron bar. When a few days
later the Jews were ordered to leave Majdan, we fled, taking
nothing with us and without even trying to find a cart.

When we heard that the Germans had burned forty Jews
alive in Lubaczów, we fled to the Russian side and arrived in
the village of Czytków.

At two in the morning, before Sukkos—we had already
put up the *sukka** in our courtyard—the Germans gave the
order that not a single Jew would be allowed in Łańcut after
four o'clock and that anyone who stayed would be killed.
People ran panic-stricken to their homes to get their things.
The rich hired carts for enormous sums of money. My father
wanted to share the hire of a cart with two neighbors, but
they did not have as much money as the peasant wanted to
charge. So we ran to the San with our bundles on our backs.

---

*The temporary "tabernacle" or booth built for Sukkos. Observant Jews take
their meals in it during the holiday.

When the order was given for all Jews to leave Łańcut for the Russian side within two hours, we tried to make our way across by boat, but the Russians would not let us get off the boats and told us to go back to the Germans. We shuttled back and forth all night long, until a few Jews collected jewelry to give to the Soviet guards; then they let us through.

My dad had fled to his sister in Kobryń before the Germans arrived in Biała Podlaska. He wanted to take us with him but my grandmother would not let him. At the last minute, when the Germans were already entering the town, Mama grabbed me and ran with me to the Russian side. I didn't see the Germans, but I did see many terrible things.

❧

Russians, Bolsheviks

The relief the Jews felt in the Soviet-occupied zone was short-lived. Stalin decided to annex the occupied Polish territories to the Soviet republics of Belorussia and Ukraine, and to this end a "plebiscite" was conducted on October 22, 1939, in the western Ukraine and Belorussia. This took the form of elections to the peoples' councils (the "soviets"). The election campaign was one-sided and accompanied by fraud and violence, especially by agents of the NKVD (the Soviet secret police). Immediately after these "elections," whose outcome had been determined in advance, the territories in question were annexed to the Soviet Union by the Supreme Soviet's edicts of November 1 and 2, 1939, and Soviet citizenship forced on the inhabitants of the area.

On September 18 the Russian tanks rolled in and we breathed a sigh of relief that the German danger had passed. The Bolsheviks made a beeline for the stores, buying up everything in sight. The whole town turned into a marketplace. Everyone was buying and selling, from rabbis and lawyers to Polish office workers and judges. When word spread that Vilna was to be handed over to the Lithuanians, the local Jews, fearing Lithuanian antisemites, began to leave for Russia. From the other direction came an influx of Jews from Polish towns wanting to leave the country. On October 27 the Lithuanians took Vilna, and the pogrom began that same day. Polish thugs joined forces with the Lithuanians, and Jews were beaten on the streets and Jewish stores robbed. Thousands were wounded. Only after three days did the Lithuanian police decide to restore order.

We had a hard time in Grzymalów, because as soon as the Polish army left the town a gang of Ukrainians started beating the Jews and robbing Jewish homes. It was two days before the Russians arrived.

Five days after we arrived in Kamień Kaszyrski, the Russian tanks drove in and the Jews heaved a sigh of relief. Stores were opened and they filled up with Russians. The Russian soldiers marched through the town all day long, singing songs, children running after them. The Jews thought the war was over.

When the Russians entered Krzeszów, the Jews came out of hiding. On the whole the Russians treated the people well. They ordered that the mills be opened and they distributed the bread. They confiscated cattle from the squires and distributed it to the poor. Bodies in the fresh graves in the middle of town were dug up and buried in the Jewish cemetery. The Bolsheviks made propaganda about how good things were in Russia. Many people enlisted in the Red Militia. When it became known that the Russians were leaving the town all the Jews fled—on foot, packages in hands.

The Bolsheviks arrived in Izbica on Thursday and the Jewish population breathed a sigh of relief. They were given a friendly welcome. Some of the young people joined the militia and wore red armbands. The Bolsheviks took the squires' cattle and carried it away on trucks. The militia helped them search for weapons. The Bolsheviks were only there for eight days. As they were leaving they advised the Jews to go with them. They said no one would harm us in Russia. About a hundred families decided to go, including us.

In Nachal the local Communists helped the Bolsheviks to search for weapons. The Poles were outraged by that. When the Bolsheviks were leaving, some Polish friends of ours warned us that the Polish population felt hostile toward the Jews because of the way the Jewish Communists had behaved and advised us to leave town as there might be acts of revenge. We told others about this, and almost all the Jews left in the direction of Rawa Ruska.

During the first days of the Russian occupation, order was maintained in Lwów by the civilian militia. Then they were replaced by the Red Militia appointed by the Bolsheviks. They grabbed people on the streets to remove barricades and fill in ditches. Only the better-dressed people were seized.

The Russians formed a militia and at first things were calm in Lesko, so the Hasidim sent my father to Bełżec to get the great rabbi. My father put him up in our house. Ten days later, when we found out that the Bolsheviks were leaving and the Germans were coming back, the rabbi said the Jews should leave town, and my father and he left for Sokal, taking only the Torah with them. I stayed behind with my mother, to rent a cart after Sukkos and get the merchandise out of the shop.

The Bolsheviks paid high prices for shoes and clothes and would pay any amount for watches. We showed them where to get leather and they ordered shoes from my father for their wives in Russia. When we found out after a week that they were leaving Hrubieszów, panic broke out among the Jews. My father rented a cart and we set off. As we were passing through a forest, our driver gave a whistle and two peasants jumped out from behind the trees. They threw us off the cart and drove away with all our belongings, even though my father begged them at least to leave him his lasts. Losing his lasts was what distressed my father most of all. "If I have my lasts," he said, "wherever I wind up I can sit down on my stool and I won't go hungry. But without my lasts I feel I've lost my hands." He left us there in the forest and returned a few hours later carrying on his back a sack of lasts and several pieces of leather that he had kept hidden in the cellar.

Upon hearing the news that the Russians had entered Łuków, we returned home. When the Russians left the town six days later I went with my father and brothers to Brest.

When we heard that the Russians had taken Chełm, we wanted to go back home, but we had to postpone our departure because my uncle's wound, which he got on the way out of Warsaw, opened up again. Shortly after that, the news reached us that Chełm had been retaken by the Germans, so we traveled to Kowel.

When we found out the Russians were leaving Węgrów, my father and grandfather decided to go to Białystok.

When the Bolsheviks announced a few days after their

arrival in Siedlce that they were pulling out, most of the Jewish population and many Poles left with them. We went too, although my father knew that as a rabbi the Bolsheviks would give him a hard time. On the way, we met Jewish refugees from many neighboring towns.

My father hesitated about crossing to the Russian side, but in the end he hired a cart and we went to Kubnów near Rawa Ruska. The Russians allowed us across the border but refused to let the peasant back. It was only my father's pleading, backed up with a box of matches, that convinced the Russian guard to let the peasant return.

I persuaded my father and brother that we should sneak across the border. Old Rabbi Wajdenfeld from Dąbrowa set out with us. When our boat was in the middle of the river, the Germans opened fire. The rabbi had a heart attack and died in my arms. We carried him ten kilometers to Sieniawa and buried him in the Jewish cemetery. At the border the Germans and Ukrainians took everything we had, but we were happy that they had let us through and that we were now in the Soviet Union.

My father secretly made his way across to the Russian side and left us behind in Kałuszyn with a friend, a shoemaker called Mendel. Then he sent a smuggler from Wołkowysk to get us. We got into his boat at night. In the middle of the lake the smuggler said he wouldn't take us any further unless we paid him more, and we had to hand over all of our money.

My father gave all our savings to a peasant to get him to smuggle us to Vilna, but instead of taking us to the Lithuanian side he drove us to the Soviet guardhouse and we were locked up in a cold cell. During the night Mama felt terrible pains, and we started hammering on the door. They took her to the hospital and she gave birth to Beniek. A policeman guarded her the whole time she was in the hospital. Then Mama was brought back to the cell together with Beniek and we were all sentenced to five years in prison as foreign spies. My father wanted to take all the blame upon himself, but no one would listen to him. They wouldn't even tell us which country we were spying for.

My father put us on a cart, for which he paid a fortune of

money, and we went to Sieniawa. But there we met thousands of Jewish refugees and we couldn't find anyplace to spend the night. It was also hard to find bread and other food. Two weeks later we moved to Sterwice near Brody, where our relatives and friends lived.

When we arrived in Rawa Ruska the town was overflowing with refugees. We slept in a cramped, dirty *beys medresh.* Later on we moved in with the *shoykhet,* who rented us a tiny room.

The sidewalks in Rawa Ruska were jammed with people and bundles, so we went to Lwów.

We arrived in Sieniawa where my uncle, a poor teacher, lived. He shared everything he had with us, his formerly rich relatives. In Sieniawa my father dealt in any merchandise he could get—flour, sugar, shoes, dollars—and two months later, when the railway line had been repaired, we moved to Lwów.

After seven weeks of wandering we arrived in Jagielnica. We had lost most of our things on the way and had spent almost all of our money. We stayed with my uncle, who owned a food store. The store was empty and no new merchandise was coming in. His tiny two-room dwelling gained eleven extra people.

We stayed close to the border because Mama thought she would hear from my father. My grandfather mourned him for days on end.

My grandfather, grandmother, two uncles, and their families were fleeing with us. On our way to the San the Germans tormented us cruelly. The peasants refused to take us in for the night or to sell us food. At night we slept in the fields until we reached Niemirów, where the crush of people was terrible because the evacuees refused to journey any further.

When we arrived in Białystok the town was full of refugees and we barely managed to find a little corner in the school.

In Białystok we found a little corner in a packed synagogue to spend the night.

In Białystok it was not easy to get into the synagogue,

which was full of refugees who did not want to let new people in. Fortunately we met some friends there.

In Białystok we met many friends from Czerniakowska Street, so we moved into the *beys medresh*, where there was not enough room on the floor. My mother and the older children slept during the day and my father and the younger ones at night.

In Białystok we couldn't find a place to stay, and we spent the night in the *beys medresh*, where people stole from each other and squabbled.

We trudged through the streets of Białystok before finding a corner in the overcrowded synagogue on Jerusalem Street.

In Białystok, my father found a room on a street called International Street, formerly Jewish Street.

There were so many refugees in Białystok that we couldn't find a place to stay, and the baby kept crying. My stepmother's arms were dropping from constantly carrying the baby and she could hardly stand on her feet. We went from house to house until finally a woman took pity on us. She lived in a tiny room with four people, and now there were eight. The baby cried during the night but my stepmother had no milk.

We couldn't find a place to stay in Białystok so we went to our relatives in Pinsk.

In Białystok we stayed in a wooden bunkhouse and froze the whole winter.

We spent the winter in Sarny at 10 Kupiecka Street. We bought firewood from our former workers, who brought it from our estate.

In Brest we stayed in an abandoned *beys medresh*, and we had to stand on line for hours in the cold to get a loaf of bread.

In Siemiatycze we could not find a place for the night, so we went on to my uncle's in Baranowicze.

Zambrów was full of refugees, and we slept in a crowded synagogue. From there we fled to Boćki, where a relative of ours was a rabbi.

In Zambrów, in a house full of refugees, there was not even space to lie down on the floor. So we went to Białystok and moved into a place run by some organization, where you had to watch your things because people were stealing from each other.

✿

In Białystok Mama started buying and selling. I washed dishes in a cheap eatery and helped her in this way.

In Białystok my father started trading. My older sister Esther would travel with him to neighboring towns to buy merchandise.

In Białystok my father traded in salt, textiles, watches—whatever he could find—and my older brother helped him. The Bolsheviks would come to our place and buy everything. My father said that this way we would easily get through the war.

My mother bought and sold, and somehow we managed. But soon the Bolsheviks started to bring in new rules. They threw people out of their homes, confiscated shops, and would not give their owners any work.

When the Bolsheviks nationalized my father's haberdashery store we had no means of survival. As a former yeshiva student, I did not know how to find a job or how to do business. We sold our clothes, but there were many people in our situation and we had few customers.

My father applied for a job as a textile specialist but was told there were no jobs for lousy bourgeois. He became a porter and earned eight rubles a day.

My father became a watchman in a factory. He earned very little but he would always bring back bread.

My father tried to get work in a shoe factory. Then he set up a workshop together with five partners.

My brother worked as a shoemaker, but we went hungry because it was hard for him to support us four in addition to his own family.

My brother worked in a sawmill and things were very hard for him, because apart from his own family he now had to support my mother and me. My mother tried her hand at buying and selling, but it went badly and she risked being imprisoned.

In Kowel my father worked in a cap makers' cooperative, but he earned so little that it was enough to buy just bread.

My mother tried to help him by buying and selling, but the antibusiness regulations were becoming stricter and stricter, so she stopped.

We worked in a shoe factory in Tołoczno, Vitebsk *oblast,*[*] but we couldn't live off that.

What my father earned in Pinsk was not enough, and the situation kept getting worse. My father wrote to his brother in America asking him for visas. Immediately after he sent the letter he was summoned by the NKVD. When he came back he said, "They're worse than the Germans."

In Siemiatycze my uncle led prayers and taught the children, even though the Bolsheviks threatened to send him to Siberia if he didn't stop. Since they were unable to do anything with my uncle, they started to punish the parents who sent their children to study with him. My uncle's family was hard up, so Mama started a business with the help of my older brother Hersh. They brought goods from Białystok and sold them in Baranowicze, and that is what both families lived on.

In Kubnów people lived mainly off of smuggling. Sugar and other food was brought in from the German side, kerosene and salt from the Russian side. There were many casualties. A German soldier shot Zelatyner and then tied a stone to his neck and dropped him through an ice hole. The Jewish community got permission from the commandant of the border guards to fish out the corpse and bury it. The whole town took part in the funeral.

We were in a difficult situation in Białystok. My sister supported us by smuggling food to Lwów. My father would have nothing to do with smuggling.

Things went well for us in Kobryń, because my father was working in a mill.

In the spring the Bolsheviks ordered the refugees to move

[*]Administrative district.

a hundred kilometers from the border, so we left Białystok and went to Iwa. The local Jews there helped us as best they could and let us onto the bread lines.

When the order came for refugees to leave Białystok, we were sent with hundreds of others to Iwa, although most people soon went their separate ways because there was nothing to live on there. My father traded in shoes and leather, and my sister was still traveling to Lwów.

When the order came for all refugees living within twenty-five kilometers of the border to move to the interior of the country, my father signed up for work in Gomel. At the station we were greeted with music, speeches, and a lavish meal and were then put up in a tiny room in a worker's hostel where there were a thousand people living and no running water. My father worked hard in the brick factory but his wages were not enough to live on. What bothered him most was that they would not give him Saturdays off. After four months, my father fled to Równe, where our friends from Włodawa lived. When my father had more or less settled himself there, my mother went to the NKVD and told them that my father had left us, and that she could not feed four children and was asking for permission to travel to relatives in the Ukraine. She was told to write out an application but for a long time there was no answer. My mother went again, and a couple of months later she received the answer that she was to go to work and should give us up to an orphanage. We quickly packed our things and fled to my father. In Równe my father worked and my mother did some buying and selling. Compared to Gomel it was paradise.

My father could not find work, so he signed up to go to Russia. He was promised a job in his profession, good wages, and a place to live. When we arrived in Gomel we were greeted with music, speeches, and a lavish meal at the station. Then we were taken to a workers' hostel where we got a tiny room with no furniture. The next day my father went to the office to ask where his workplace was, but there was no work and they advised us to go to the *kolkhoz*.[*] We worked in the

[*] Collective farm.

fields beginning at dawn and into the night for a ration of bread, a few potatoes, and a little soup, and we were constantly hungry. Once a week the children would get some milk. After a few weeks the manager of the farm told us he had no more work for us and we would have to go back to town. We were facing starvation, so we decided to return to Białystok. We were afraid of the NKVD men, so Mama, my sister, and our youngest brother got into one train car and I and my father and older brother into another. With God's help we made it to Białystok. Again we moved into the synagogue, and my father, older sister, and brother started to buy and sell.

The Russians made it known that workers were needed in the interior of the country and advised us to volunteer—if not, they would take us by force. We volunteered.

We arrived in Zolotonosha in Poltava province. Most of the inhabitants were Jews, including the president, Yarshevsky. We were greeted with music at the station, and we were given something to eat and some clothes. Appeals were posted on the shops to allow refugees in without waiting on line. Two weeks later we were sent to a nearby *kolkhoz*. It had once belonged to Jews but only forty Jewish families, who occupied the top positions, remained there. The executive office was in a former synagogue. My father did not have the strength to work in the fields so he was put in a home for the disabled. But the food there was not kosher and my father took us back to Kowel. "So that's how the refugees show their gratitude to Russia for the warm welcome. The Russians will feel offended and take revenge on them," said Yarshevsky, the town president.

We arrived in the town of Azditish, where only Jews lived and where they had a committee for assistance to refugees. For four months we were treated well, but then some NKVD officials came from Moscow and investigated everyone. My father hid, but in the end they caught all the refugees and loaded us onto a train. It was wintertime and there were little heating stoves burning in the train. We were taken to the city of Gorky, but three months later the NKVD officials appeared again. Russia's a big place, they said, and anyone who doesn't volunteer to go will be sent to Siberia with the criminals. We volunteered and were taken to Pravdinsk. There was a paper factory there and the refugees were ordered to carry two-cubic-meter blocks of wood. My father would bring back bread from the factory and my mother stood on line for other food. Sometimes a thousand people were standing on line. The Russian Jews would give my mother their place on line, saying we had suffered enough through the war. They would even bring bread to our house and candy for the children. The factory had an enormous canteen for the workers, but the food was not kosher so my father could not eat there. After three months, notices appeared on walls saying that refugees should not be given any special treatment since they were already Soviet citizens. From then on we stood on line like everyone else. Often there were fights, and sometimes you could wait all night and leave without any bread.

My father and grandfather worked. Women and children would stand on line all night long for bread, sugar, and other food.

We children used to stand on line for nights and would often come back at dawn without bread.

We wanted to go back to Volhynia, but the road led through Moscow. To get to Moscow you had to have permission from the commandant, but anyone asking for it was sent to Siberia. We sold a few things and illegally bought tickets for a boat, paying five rubles extra for each ticket. In Moscow we spent the night on the street. The shop windows were full of everything, even foreign goods—as in Poland before the war. In Kiev many refugees were sleeping on the streets, and the NKVD made a raid in the night. "You want to go to Volhynia? By all means." We and thousands of others were surrounded by a cordon of guards. One of the refugees tried to hang himself, and they just managed to save him. That same night we were loaded onto a train. We breathed a sigh of relief when the train left Shepetovka behind. Now we could get sugar and bread. Now we could live.

Many young people applied to work in Russia. They were given a rousing send-off but after a few months they came back.

Mama did not know how to manage, so she put our names

down as volunteers to go to Russia. But before we left, my brother Abram saw a friend from Bielsko on the street, who said our father was in Białystok looking for us. My father came running to us and kissed us. He had been wounded in battle, had been in the hospital, and the Russians had taken him prisoner together with other officers, but he had escaped from the camp. We went with my father of our own free will to the Kherson district. My father got a job there as a game-keeper but he was very weak after his experiences at the front and in the POW camp. He caught cold in the forest and fell very ill. The hospital told him it was tuberculosis. Since he was unfit for work they sent us to Lwów.

In Lwów, the administration consisted of Russians, Ukrainians, and Jews, mostly young ones. The Jews had the lower positions while the Russians and the Ukrainians were in the higher ones. The refugees bought and sold for a living.

In Lwów we survived mainly by standing for hours on line, buying things and then selling them on the black market.

In Lwów our family bought and sold. We children helped our parents. We traded in everything: sugar, wine, vodka, tex-tiles.

In Lwów a friend of my father's made soap. It looked like clay, and yet people couldn't buy it fast enough. I delivered this soap to the merchants.

One day my father came back from town with the news that walking around with packages was out, because agents were searching people on the street. I and my younger sister Bela, who was ten, told him to give the packages to us, be-cause they did not search children. My father showed us where to buy and sell, and we became the mainstays of the family.

My father traded in flour, my mother traveled to small towns to buy goods and food, and I sold cigarettes. The police picked me up several times and wanted to know where I got my goods from. I said it was from people I ran into on the street. They threatened to deport me to Siberia.

Once my brother and I were caught on the tram with twelve liters of vodka. On the way to the police station I escaped and ran to Benjamin Filer, who had given us the goods. He went to the police with an NKVD man he knew and for two hundred rubles my brother was released.

One time my sister was caught carrying soap. They held her at the police station all night and beat her to get her to say where we lived. My sister did not tell them, but from then on my father was afraid to do any selling, and once again we had nothing to eat.

My father began dealing in leather and shoes. They arrested him and threatened to send him to Siberia. My mother sold flour, but we went hungry because she earned so little.

It was not easy to do business in Lwów. A friend of ours from Rozwadów, Mr. Kirszenbojm, was sentenced to five years in prison because they found a dollar on him. Another friend got five years for dealing in matches.

My father started working for a saddler but his earnings kept falling. My stepmother was a good dressmaker, but there was no fabric, thread, or needles. My Uncle Leib was caught doing business and was deported to Siberia.

They arrested my father and confiscated his goods. Three days later he came back, but he had a heart attack that same night and we didn't let him do any more business. I found a few brushes and a can of shoe polish and went to town carrying a little box. I got two, three, sometimes five rubles for shining shoes. I earned sixty rubles a day, even a hundred on holidays.

My father got together with several *shoykhets* and set up a business. My older brother carried foodstuffs to the larger towns, and my other brother and sister helped him. My father complained about the constant new restrictions on the kosher meat business but said he would never agree to sell *treyf.*[*]

My father went from village to village, slaughtering cattle for Jews. He was warned that if they caught him doing ritual slaughtering he would be sent to Siberia. Mama asked him to

[*]Nonkosher food.

stop, but her income was not enough to keep us and my father went on working. One day he was caught in the slaughter-house and they confiscated his calves, but on the way to the militia station he managed to bribe a guard. My father stopped doing it but was still under surveillance. My mother was not able to do business either because they were constantly search-ing our house, and things were very bad for us.

My father took foodstuffs to Przemyśl and brought back goods for the peasants, and that's what we lived on. We had papers for going to America, where my father had been promised a job as rabbi.

We wanted to go to America or Palestine, where we had relatives. To take care of the formalities we moved to Lwów and rented a small apartment. My father taught several chil-dren, and on Saturdays prayers were held in our house, and that is what we lived on.

Relatives found a furnished apartment for us. During the day older children would come, and with the shutters closed my father would teach them from the Holy Books, and in the evening the older men would sit over the books with him. The NKVD found out about it and every day at dawn he was taken for interrogation and threatened with Siberia. Every step he took was watched and people avoided him on the street. My mother cried and asked him to stop, but he went on teaching.

In Lwów thousands of Jews were roaming the streets. Since we had nothing to live on, we went to Bolerów, where we had relatives. We supported ourselves there for six months by buying and selling.

Unable to find a place to stay in Lwów, which was full of refugees from all over Poland, we moved to Strzyżów, where my father's sister lived and where my uncle was president of the Jewish community. Through my uncle, my father got to know a baker who supplied bread to the army, and he got a job delivering wood to the bakery. I and my older brother traveled to Lwów and traded in vodka and almonds.

Since we had nothing to wear, Mama decided to go back to Rozwadów for the things she left with our Christian neighbors. She went, but could not return, even though my father paid smugglers to bring her back.

In February, the mass arrests began in Lwów. Social activists, Bundists,[*] Zionists, and officers' wives—twenty-five thousand people—were deported to Siberia.

In Nowogródek they arrested former legionnaires who had received land from the government, as well as the families of policemen, officers, and officials. They also arrested the merchant Akiva Kasmaj along with his sixty-year-old brother and his elderly mother, as well as the Revisionist Benjamin Efron, accused of arguing with the Communists, and Kahan the tailor, who had once made uniforms for Polish officers.

In Lwów they divided the streets into blocks and the commandant of each block made sure that no one got out of voting. The sick had ballot boxes brought to their beds. You voted for a fixed slate that had neither Poles nor Jews on it.

In Nowogródek they gave out free rolls and candy at the voting stations. People who did not vote or who spoke disapprovingly of the elections were arrested and deported a few days later. The Labor Office chief was a Communist sent from Russia, and his deputies were a teacher called Nacumowski and someone named Szapiro. The bourgeois did not get work. Landowners got internal passports marked with the number 13; other suspicious people got 11's and were not entitled to live in category I and II towns. Former officials, social activists, and rabbis were given three-month passports. One synagogue was used as a warehouse, the other for workshops. One of the churches was converted into a community center and cinema. The young people relished the freedom from religious taboos.

In Choroszów people were forced to participate in the

---

[*]Members of the Bund, a Jewish socialist organization founded in Russia in 1897.

elections and to vote for the Ukrainian candidate, but very many Jews, particularly religious ones, did not vote.

My father did not vote, but we were not afraid that anything would happen to us, since Boćki was a small town where power was in the hands of the local Communists.

My father avoided ceremonies and meetings, where they always sang Stalin's praises. But he was not fired from his job, because he was an excellent bookkeeper and they could not manage without him.

In the winter of 1940 everyone was urged to accept Soviet passports, and people were forced to move to small towns at least a hundred kilometers from the border.

In April the passport decree was issued, but even people who accepted them did not receive full citizens' rights and were deported to small towns.

My father did not take part in the elections and would not accept a Soviet passport. He said the Soviet air was stifling him.

When they started urging people to accept Soviet citizenship, my father refused. The Bełżec rebbe did not want to become a Soviet citizen either.

My father was fired from his job as a porter because he did not accept a Soviet passport, so he started traveling to Kowel to sell.

My parents refused to accept Soviet citizenship for fear that they would not be able to leave Russia. As a result, my father was fired and our situation became terrible. Regardless of the danger, my mother traveled to Równe to get merchandise that she sold for us to survive.

When we had to decide whether to accept Soviet passports, my parents decided not to since that would mean remaining in Russia forever.

My parents did not want to become Soviet citizens so that they would not lose the chance of returning home after the war.

Mama did not want to accept Soviet citizenship because people said we would never be able to leave Russia and see our father again.

When my father was summoned to the police station and asked whether he wanted to become a Soviet citizen, he said no. They threatened to send him back to the Germans. Other refugees were also asked where they wanted to go. Some said to relatives in America, others to Palestine.

My father would not hear of Soviet citizenship because he was afraid we would not be able to leave for America.

We were not given Soviet passports because, being a rabbi, my father was viewed as an unproductive element.

One day my father heard that anyone without a passport would be sent to Siberia, and we wanted to leave Niemirów. But our relatives insisted that we stay.

One day my father told us they were registering people to return to Poland and that anyone who did not register had to become a Soviet citizen. My parents decided to register.

One day my father came home in a good mood and said they had opened an office on the main street and were registering people who wanted to go back home, or to Lithuania if they had relatives there. Mama was very happy and we put our names down to go to Vilna, where my oldest sister lived.

In April and May they held a registration in Białystok of people who wanted to go back to the German side.

At first people distrusted the registration and only a few families, mainly Christian, put their names down. But when the first group actually was taken over to the German side we decided to register.

My father would not accept a Soviet passport and was one of the first to apply to return when registration began.

My father did not want a Soviet passport and, like all our neighbors from the synagogue, registered to go back home.

My father saw that life in the Soviet Union was getting more and more difficult and decided to register us to go back home.

Our situation was so bad that when the registration was announced Mama put our names down to go back home.

My father did not want a Soviet passport, and my mother persuaded him to register us to go back, because we were constantly threatened with starvation.

My father got a three-month passport, but he could not earn anything and our whole family was starving, so he registered us to return to Warsaw.

My father applied to go back to Warsaw, thinking that somehow he would manage in a large city.

My father and brothers registered to go back to Warsaw, thinking it would be easier to leave the country from there.

My father was afraid it would be impossible to get out of Russia and wanted to return to the German side in order to leave for America from there.

My father registered us to go to America, to our relatives.

We registered to go to Lithuania, thinking that from there we would be able to get to Palestine.

My parents decided to return to Łódź because they had left my seven-year-old sister Chaya there with my grandparents.

When they started registering people who wanted to go back to the German occupation zone, my father put his name down immediately because Mama was there.

My father registered us because news was coming from the other side that the situation had improved and that people were earning enough to live on, while here things were getting worse and worse.

My father registered to go home because he had heard that Jews had returned to Pułtusk and that you could earn a living again.

We did not want to become Soviet citizens and, since the news from the German zone was that life there was back to normal, we registered to leave.

My father could not get used to the new order and wanted to go back home, where he had money and goods buried in the cellar.

We registered, like many other Jews. One of the main reasons was the lack of kosher food.

The NKVD asked, "Do you want to go back to the Germans or stay in Russia?" We said we wanted to go back home despite the fact the Germans were there.

In Kiev the Ukrainians, the Jews, and the Poles all wanted to go back home, even though it was under German rule.

We traveled to Baranowicze, where the German commission was, and we registered to go back home.

When they announced the registration for returning to German-occupied territory, my parents decided to register, especially since they did not believe the Germans would let the Jews back in again.

We did not want to stay in Russia. We just wanted to wait out the war in a little town where things were relatively quiet. We didn't go and register because we didn't want to go back to the Germans.

My father did not accept Soviet citizenship but did not want to register to go to the German side.

My father didn't go anywhere, either to vote or to register.

My father did not register us to go back to the Germans; he said it was a trap.

My father was stopped at the station on his way to Kowel with his goods. When they ordered him to show his passport, he said he didn't have one because he had registered to go to Łódź where his child was. He was arrested and deported, no one knew where to.

My brother, who used to travel from Siedlce smuggling leather and fabrics across the border, said that our father wanted us to go back to him. The first time he took twelve-year-old Noah and seven-year-old Sara and the second time ten-year-old Shlomo. On the third journey, the NKVD men caught him and he was unable to come for me.

On the twenty-ninth of June the blackout order was issued. People in town said the reason for the blackout was the war with Romania, but in fact the dark evenings were used to purge undesirable elements.

The Longest Journey

In early 1940 the NKVD began a campaign of mass arrests and mass exile of Polish citizens into the Soviet hinterland. The first deportation was conducted in February, the second in April, and the third in June. The number of people sent into exile is still debated. Soviet documents indicate that in February 1940 alone some 140 thousand Polish citizens were exiled, while Polish sources put the number at about 250 thousand. The total number of Polish citizens exiled is estimated by Polish sources to have been about 1.5 to 1.7 million, among them nearly half a million Jews, while a secret memorandum sent by the Soviet commissar for internal affairs to Stalin in May 1944 sets the number of Polish citizens under arrest or exiled in the Soviet Union as of August 1941 at only 389,382. During the exile period, the Soviet authorities also moved away from the border those refugees who had come from the west. They were encouraged to voluntarily migrate deeper into the Soviet Union and to work there in industrial plants. The volunteers were predominantly Jewish.

On Friday evening there was a knock on our door. Mama ran to open it, thinking my father had returned. In walked four NKVD men. When Mama asked what they wanted, they said, "You're going to your husband." Mama was happy and told us to get dressed quickly.

On Friday evening NKVD men knocked on our door. They said we should go with them to explain why we wanted to go back to Biłgoraj and told us to take our things with us. When my father asked why we needed our things, they said we could leave them behind.

On Friday evening armed NKVD men came into our home and ordered us to pack our things, saying we were going to Warsaw.

One night some NKVD men appeared and said a truck was waiting for us and they were sending us back home.

On June 28, in the night, armed NKVD men knocked on our door. They beamed searchlights and began pushing us to hurry up and get dressed. When my uncle asked where we were going, they said they were sending us to the Germans.

On Friday at midnight there was a violent knocking on the door and NKVD men with revolvers drawn ordered us to get dressed quickly.

At two o'clock in the morning four NKVD men came in, carrying revolvers. One stood by the door, another by the window, and they informed us that we were going to Germany.

At three in the morning there was a knock on our door. Two NKVD men came in along with two soldiers with rifles, and they ordered us to pack our things.

One night several soldiers came in and ordered us to get dressed and pack our things, after which they took us by truck to the station.

On Friday, in the night, we were woken up by NKVD men. They would not let us pack anything, but the Jewish militiaman who was with them allowed us to take a few things.

One day an NKVD official, a Jew, appeared at our house and asked to see our papers. Then NKVD men came in the night with the same official, who this time refused to speak Yiddish to us, and we were taken to the station.

In the middle of the night there was a knock on our door. Soldiers with rifles were standing by the window. They said we were going to Baranowicze where an exchange of civilians was taking place. In the marketplace we met people from Wyszków and Międzyrzec. We were taken to the station in trucks.

On June 28, in the middle of the night, NKVD men surrounded our house and marched us to the station. They said we were going to Lida because refugees were fleeing Iwa. But in Lida they would not let us out and just hitched us to a long freight train crammed with people. In Mołodeczno we were taken off the train and put onto broad-gauge cars. My sister stayed behind because she was traveling on business at the time.

My brother came running from the sawmill with the news that all refugees were to be transported to Białystok. We packed our things, and indeed that same night the NKVD came and took us to the sawmill, where all the refugees were loaded onto a freight train, fifty to a car.

On Friday, June 28, my father arrived with a freight-car-load of wood. We children helped him to unload it. When we had finished, NKVD men came and told us to clean the car. That same night two policemen with revolvers drawn knocked on our door. My father and older brother hid in the attic. When asked where my father was, we said he had gone to Stryj on business, but when they told us to get dressed and take our things, my father and brother came out of hiding. The policemen got very angry and would not allow us to take anything with us. We were bundled into the freight car that we had cleaned that morning. The car was sealed and we were taken to Stryj, where other cars were coupled on.

On Friday, at one in the morning, NKVD men came to our house and announced they were sending us to the Germans. We cried and said we wanted to stay, but it was no use. They took us to the station and locked us in a freight car guarded by a policeman with a rifle.

On Friday, in the night, we were awakened by gun butts pounding on the door. My brother and I were terrified. When my father refused to open, they began to shoot. My uncle, white as a sheet, came into our room and told us to open the door. We were not allowed to take anything with us. The street was black with people, the women were crying.

One Friday night they started pounding on the door with the butts of their guns. We children hid in the darkest corner. Russian soldiers came in and ordered us to get dressed quick-ly. They took us to the marketplace, where a crowd of people was already standing. We heard shots. At dawn they took us all to the station and loaded us into freight cars.

One night an NKVD agent arrived at our house and shouted that they would send us to Siberia. We cried as we told him what we had already been through. He was clearly moved and left us under house arrest. But later another NKVD agent came and said, "You want to go to the Germans? Then you'll go." And he took us to the station, where there was already a large group of refugees. The train cars were locked and the armed guards were not letting anyone out.

On Friday, in the night, the NKVD men came and took us to the station. My older sister was in Białystok at the time. When she returned to Kowel and saw what had happened, she went to the NKVD and asked them to send her to us. They sent her all right, but to the other end of Russia, and we had no news of her for a very long time.

On Friday evening the NKVD surrounded the streets and told us to pack our things.

On Friday evening NKVD men appeared. They only allowed us to pack a few small things, then drove us by truck to the station.

One Friday evening we were told to get dressed. We were not allowed to take anything.

On Friday, in the night, NKVD men made a thorough search of our house, then took us to the station.

One Friday night NKVD men ordered everyone living in the synagogue to pack their things, and they took us to the station.

One night NKVD men appeared in our synagogue and told everyone to go to the station.

One night we were all taken out of the jail and loaded onto freight cars.

On Friday, in the night, NKVD men took us to the station, where we met thousands of people.

A group of NKVD men knocked at our door. They ordered us to pack our things and took us by cart to the railway station.

One Friday night NKVD men arrived and drove us by cart

to Przemyśl. My father and older brother went on foot because it was the Sabbath.

On Saturday morning NKVD men came to our house and informed us that we were going to Warsaw.

On Saturday, at six in the morning, NKVD men searched our house. They spent a long time looking over my father's books. My father tried to explain what they meant, but they could not understand much. They took the books and transported us to the station, where we found thousands of people.

On June 29, 1940, NKVD men came to us in the night and ordered us to get dressed, saying we were going back to Germany.

On June 29, 1940, we were arrested and taken by cart to the station, where fifty train cars were standing, crammed with people.

On Saturday, June 29, NKVD men came in and told us to be ready to leave within half an hour.

They ordered us to pack up our things within fifteen minutes.

In Iwa the refugees were arrested on June 29. My oldest sister stayed behind because she was near Pinsk at the time.

On June 29, 1940, they arrested our family like bandits.

On June 30, 1940, NKVD men surrounded the houses. They allowed each family to take one hundred kilos of luggage.

They did not allow me to take my books with me.

My parents were arrested, but I was not. Papa and Mama wanted me to stay with my uncle in Kobryń, but I cried bitterly and finally got myself into their train car.

The NKVD did not come to our house and we thought they had forgotten us. They came on the third day, saying they had had the wrong address and because of that we had to travel with strangers since all of our friends had already gone.

❁

They loaded us into dark train cars.

They loaded us into train cars with no windows.

They loaded us into cramped, dirty cars.

They packed us into freight cars, which they then sealed.

They put us into freight cars, forty people to a car with their luggage. It was a terrible squeeze.

They loaded us into freight cars, forty-five people to a car.

They loaded us into cars, fifty people to a car.

There were between fifty and sixty people in each car.

They took us to the station by truck and crammed us into a train car that had seventy people in it.

They packed us in, eighty people to a car, and sealed the doors.

They packed us in, ninety people to a car.

They packed us into cars that were cramped and dirty and we lay on top of each other.

They loaded us onto a train where there were already two thousand people.

The train had fifty cars. Most of the people on the train were Jews, the rest Poles.

They locked us into freight cars and did not give us any water or bread.

They kept us for twenty-four hours without giving us anything to eat or drink.

The whole of Saturday they kept us in that cramped, stuffy place without water or food.

We stood at the station all day and all night without bread and water.

We stood for twenty-four hours in the station and were given nothing to eat or drink.

The cars were sealed and we stood in the station for two days and two nights.

For two days and two nights they kept us in the station in sealed cars with nothing to eat or drink.

We were standing in Stryj for two days.

The train was standing from Friday to Sunday, and we were given nothing to eat or drink.

The cars were locked, and for three days they kept us in the station without food or drink. We cried out, but it was no use.

The train was standing for three days. We were given nothing to eat or drink and our friends were not allowed to give us packages. We suffered most from thirst.

We cried and shouted for something to drink.

They gave us nothing to eat or drink and no one was allowed in to us.

In the night, the train set off.

After twenty-four hours, the train set off.

After a whole day and night, during which we were given nothing to eat or drink, the train set off.

After two days the train moved off.

On Sunday the train set off.

After three days the train set off.

The train set off, no one knew where to.

When the train set off we were happy, because we were sure we were going back home.

We were in a good mood because we were expecting to see Mama in a few hours.

We thought they were taking us home, and my father reckoned we would be there in five or six hours, but when a night passed and then a day we realized we were traveling to the heart of Russia.

We thought we were going home, and only after some time did we realize that we had been deported to Russia.

Everyone started to cry. When we children saw the grownups weeping we began crying even louder.

In Lwów the train stopped and more cars were coupled on.

In Równe our train was hitched to another and an enormous convoy set off.

We went through Dubno, Równe, Shepetovka, and Kiev. At the big stations they allowed us to get out for water and to buy bread. In Kiev we bought a six-kilo loaf from a Jewish woman, who whispered to my father that she would happily give the exiles bread for nothing but she was not allowed to. She asked my father to share it with others.

In Kiev we stopped for a few hours and the local Jews brought us white challahs hidden under their coats.

In Kiev the train stopped for a few hours, but the guards would not let the local Jews near the train to bring us food.

In Kiev the local Jews wanted to give us food but the guards would not let them.

We traveled in sealed cars, and people bringing food for us at the station were not allowed near the train.

At the stations we saw other jam-packed trains, and Mama called me to the window, saying, "Look and see if your father's there."

Instead of four hours from Lwów to Rozwadów, we traveled long nights and days in a dirty, stuffy car.

We did not know where we were going. My father looked through a crack and tried to guess our direction. My mother was in despair.

The longer we traveled, the more convinced we became that they were taking us to Siberia.

My mother and the other women were wringing their hands over our unknown future.

I remember a Yiddish song that the children sang on the train: "Mama, I want to remember who I am and where I come from and who my parents were. Mama, this is no country for me."

The car door was locked and guarded by soldiers with rifles.

We started to cry and to bang on the door with our fists.

The children were crying and shouting for food.

It was impossible to quiet our baby down, even though I dandled her and rocked her. She was so hungry that she sucked on my fingers.

At one of the stations, desperate parents broke down the door, but soldiers prodded everyone back into the car with their rifles. Only then did we get some soup and half a kilo of bread.

We got half a kilo of bread during the day and a little soup at night.

We each got a piece of bread and a little watery soup.

In the daytime we each got a piece of bread and in the night some soup.

We got a thin slice of bread, and in the night some watery soup.

We got a piece of black bread that was so hard even water would not soften it.

We were hungry because apart from a piece of bread and a little soup we got nothing.

Even though we were famished, my father would not allow us to eat *treyf* soup, and we lived on bread and water through the whole journey.

We received four hundred grams of bread daily, and soup— which we did not eat because it was *treyf*.

My father would not eat the soup because it was *treyf*, and throughout the whole month of our journey he ate nothing apart from bread and water.

We got bread, and watery soup that my father would not touch.

We got a piece of bread and a little soup once a day, but my father ate only bread with water. We tried in vain to persuade him.

My grandfather could hardly stand on his feet, but he refused to eat the soup because it was not kosher and he ate only bread with cold water.

Once a day we got a piece of bread and a little soup, which my father would not let us eat because he thought it was *treyf*. He was allowed out at the station under guard to fetch hot water.

We got a piece of bread and a little soup. My father was not allowed to get off at the station to fetch a little warm water for the baby.

They gave us bread once a day, and a little watery soup.

Every two days we got a piece of bread and a little soup.

We got bread and hot water.

We got just enough food not to die of starvation.

We journeyed for several weeks. The train would stop for hours, but only in fields.

Whenever the train stopped at a station, we children would sneak out onto the platform and beg in the refreshment bar. We would be given customers' scraps, and we soaked the pieces of old bread in hot water.

The train car had only tiny windows, as in a prison. We children would smile at the Russians through those windows. We couldn't speak their language, but the Russians were touched by our smiles and allowed us to get off at the station to buy something to eat. We would run into the fields too and pick flowers to brighten up our dirty cars.

The train car had no toilet. Children relieved themselves through the window; grown-ups were let out at stations under escort.

The car was cramped and dirty, and it stank. Little children relieved themselves through the grated windows, while the grown-ups would suffer as they waited for the next station to be taken to the toilet under guard.

During the two-week journey we were only let out twice for fifteen minutes. We had to relieve ourselves in the car.

We were not let out of the train car. We used a hole in the floor to relieve ourselves.

We were not let out of the car. We relieved ourselves through an opening in the floor.

We were ashamed to relieve ourselves in the car and we broke down the door.

It was hard to stand the sweltering heat in the car, and there was no toilet.

There was no toilet, and the air in the car was terrible.

We almost suffocated from the stench. Mama had some drops that saved her from fainting.

The worst thing was the lack of a toilet. People relieved themselves in public through a hole in the car floor. At first people were very ashamed, especially the women. Then everyone got used to it.

The journey was long and terrible.

We traveled for several weeks without getting out of the car.

We traveled like cattle.

It was horribly stuffy. Many people fainted and there was nothing we could use to bring them to.

The crush inside the car was awful, and there was no water to revive the people who passed out.

People fainted and could not regain consciousness because there was no water.

They would give us pieces of moldy bread that made everyone sick. The car had a hole in the floor instead of a toilet, but because everybody was sick it was difficult to push your way through to it, and many children relieved themselves on the floor. We were choking from the stench and there was always someone fainting.

After a week we all came down with dysentery and there was always a line of people waiting for the hole. The children could not hold it in and relieved themselves in the car. The stench was dreadful. The women passed out and there was nothing to revive them with. Nobody listened when we shouted for help.

Many people had dysentery and there were fights to get to the hole in the floor. We children dug our own hole with a little knife.

Almost everyone in the car was sick with dysentery, but instead of a toilet we had a hole in the floor. The place was filthy, and the air in the car was deadly. At the stations we begged to be let out but our pleas fell on deaf ears.

Many people were sick but the guards didn't want to hear about it. They said that if we died there would just be a few "Polish squires" fewer.

Two people died in our car.

Several people died, and we demanded that the bodies be taken away, but the guards pretended not to hear. It was only when we started to force open the door at a station that NKVD men appeared and took away the dead.

Several people died. The train stopped in a field and they were buried near the railway embankment.

My six-year-old sister Leah fell sick with scarlet fever and everyone started screaming that the other children would get infected. The NKVD men wanted to take her away, but Mama would not let them. After a lot of squabbling and tears, Mama was allowed to get off with the child while we continued on our journey.

Mama fell ill. A doctor who was traveling in our car said she had brain fever. She was taken away on a stretcher, unconscious. We begged to be allowed to stay with her, but in vain, and we traveled on.

After two weeks of traveling we arrived in Archangelsk and then were taken ninety kilometers farther by truck. We spent the night in a *posiolok** where they gave us fish-scale soup and at four in the morning told us to wade across a river up to our necks in water. On the other bank we were picked up by barge.

In Archangelsk we were let off the train, then we were loaded onto trucks and taken to a forest in the Kargopol district, *posiolok* number 15.

We arrived in Archangelsk *oblast, posiolok* Maldinsh, Plesetsk region.

After two weeks we arrived in Sverdlovsk. From there we were taken in boats to Berezniki, where we slept out in the open and could not recognize ourselves in the morning, so badly were we bitten by mosquitoes. The next boat took us to Cherdyn and from there we were taken by truck to the *posiolok*. Nearby was a Ukrainian *posiolok* and farther on a Russian labor camp.

After two weeks we arrived at Tavda station on the river of the same name. There we were loaded onto barges, and two days we later disembarked in a forest in the Tabory district. The *posiolok* was called Chasha.

---

*Settlement or colony, here penal colony (plural *posiolki*).

After three weeks of hellish travel we arrived in Tavda. From there we were taken by truck to the forest, to the sawmill.

We were let off the train at Tavda station. From there we boarded a barge and continued our journey, during which we were given only salt herring to eat. After we got off the barge, we were walked the whole day through bogs and sand. Our feet were bloody. We arrived at *posiolok* Chasha, district of Tabory, Sverdlovsk *oblast*.

Our train took us to Tavda, and from there we sailed by river to a camp in Tos, Sverdlovsk *oblast*, Tabory district.

When we arrived in Tavda, they loaded us onto a small freight barge, which did not have much space for people. We were crammed in like cattle and for five days we sailed almost without food. People were passing out. Mosquitoes bit us all the time and children cried, all swollen. The guards teased us: "You'll never see Warsaw again." When we disembarked, some of the women had to be carried off. Enfeebled men keeled over and into the water. The NKVD men laughed and said that this was the first Russian bath for the "Polish squires." The whole day we walked through mud; we could hardly pull our feet out of it.

After fifteen days we arrived in Chelyabinsk. There we loaded our things onto carts and walked behind them for twenty kilometers to a town called Kopeisk, where we were put up in barracks.

We traveled for eighteen days to Yoshkar-Ola station, then were taken in carts to a boggy forest where we could hear wild animals howling in the night.

After eighteen days our train arrived in Siberia. On the way we found out that in the last car were Uncle Meir and his fif-teen-year-old son Motl, who used to live in a village near Przemyśl.

After three weeks—just when we were starting to think that the journey would never end—they opened the doors and told us to get out.

After three weeks we stopped near Troitsk, then walked the whole day to Vostochnaya.

We traveled for three weeks. We stopped in Troitsk district, Altaisky Krai, and walked the whole day from the station to the *posiolok*.

It was Altaisky Krai, Troitsk district. We were loaded onto carts and rode through the forest all night and all day.

For three weeks we journeyed, cramped and dirty, until we got to Vologda. Then we walked through dense forest with undergrowth slashing our legs.

After three weeks we got out in Kotlas. There we were told to board two barges, but there were several thousand of us and we could not all fit. They threatened to throw us on by force without our bags if we were not all on the barges within five minutes. Panic ensued—people trampled each other and pushed each other into the water. Several children drowned. For a day and a half we sailed down the Dvina to the village of Shevtery. From there the men went on foot while the women and children traveled on sledges drawn by a tractor. At one point a sledge tipped over and a woman from Wieluń was killed.

After three weeks we arrived in Chet, and from there they took us to the forest.

After three weeks we arrived at the Tomsk-Domashny station.

We crossed the Volga and the Yenisei and, after a journey of twenty-three days, found ourselves in Krasnoyarsky Krai. Our things were taken by cart while we walked for a day and a half through forest to *posiolok* Verkh Bazaira.

On July 23 the train stopped at Tyumen station, Omsk *oblast*. For three days they kept us out in the open. Then they loaded us onto barges and we sailed for two weeks on the River Konda. We disembarked in a forest, in a place called Verkhny Barak.

We traveled for four weeks and arrived in Vologda *oblast*.

We traveled for four weeks. They let us off the train in Asino, Sverdlovsk *oblast*.

At Asino three thousand people got out of the cars, many of them sick and weak. One doctor from Warsaw died. We were given two hundred grams of bread a day. The women cried because they could not feed their children.

Asino was the end of the railway line. It was three hundred kilometers to the nearest settlement. We were loaded onto a ship. It was supposed to hold seven hundred people but twenty-five hundred were loaded on. We lay on top of each other. For three days we sailed down a wide river, forests stretching out on either side, and occasionally we would see some barracks. There was no bread; we were fed herrings, and many people fell ill. We disembarked in Teguldet.

After a month we arrived in Asino, and from there we were taken by barge to Teguldet. Then we walked thirty-five kilometers to a place called Chet.

We were sent to Chet, out in the taiga. The richer ones traveled by cart, the poor on foot. Even in Russia money meant a lot.

We stopped in Asino and were sent to various *posiolki* in the taiga.

After four weeks we arrived at the station of Novaya Lala, Sverdlovsk *oblast,* and were taken on foot to *posiolok* number 54.

After four weeks we got off the train and went on foot to a *posiolok* in the forest.

After a month we arrived in Arkhangelsk, and from there we were marched to *posiolok* Berezovsk.

Afer a month we arrived in the Kamyshlovsk district, Sverdlovsk *oblast,* and were marched to *posiolok* number 35.

After a month we came to a stop in open fields. We were taken on foot to a river, and a small ship took us to Syktyvkar in the Komi Republic.

We got off the train seventy kilometers from Syktyvkar and were taken to the *posiolki* by tractors.

We arrived in the town of Salamadza, Kartayol district, in the Komi Republic.

After long weeks of traveling we arrived in the Komi ASSR.[*]

We spent six weeks in the train car. The station where we stopped was called Asino. Then we sailed for two days and

---

[*]Autonomous Soviet Socialist Republic.

two nights on a river hemmed in on both sides by dense forests. Our place of exile was called Nikaneyev.

We spent six weeks traveling to Asino, and from there went by boat to Teguldet. Our things were then loaded onto carts and we walked along behind them through the forest. The carts had to ride over planks because the ground was so soggy.

For six weeks we rode, hungry, louse-infested, and without a change of underwear, and then arrived in the Sverdlovsk *oblast,* Agarim district, *posiolok* number 67.

For six weeks we traveled, dirty, louse-infested, and hungry, until we got to Novosibirsk *oblast,* to a *posiolok* in the forest where there was not a single house.

For six weeks we never left the train car, and we were exiled to one of the bleakest, wildest parts of Siberia.

After two months we arrived in Novosibirsk, where you could get bread, sugar, and fruit, but we were sent further out, to Tomsk. There we were loaded onto a barge, and three days later we arrived at a *posiolok* deep in the taiga.

The journey was endless. We got out of the train in Tomsk, where they loaded us onto barges.

We went through Ufa, Omsk, Novosibirsk, and Tomsk.

We were let off at Teshma station in the Sverdlovsk *oblast.*

We were turned off the train at Cheryomushniki station in the Novosibirsk *oblast.*

The train stopped in Krasnoyarski Krai.

The train stopped at Oshchepkovo station. The surrounding area was completely wild.

After many weeks the train stopped in a dense forest.

After we got off the train, we walked for a long time before we got to *posiolok* number 25. The barracks stood there in the middle of the forest.

We were taken in trucks to a *posiolok* deep in the forest.

We arrived at a place called Pashta Nizhnaya Kirzha, Royaminka district. It was in dense forest, surrounded by barbed wire, with a guardbox at each corner.

The train stopped at Vartoga station next to a huge forest. The Bolsheviks told us, "You're bourgeois, and you'll work here till you die."

❁

Our *posiolok* was in Vologda *oblast*.

Our *posiolok* was in Novosibirsk *oblast*, Seroi region.

Our *posiolok* was in the Krasnodar *oblast*.

Our camp was in Krasnouralsk, in the Sverdlovsk *oblast*.

Our *posiolok* was deep in the forest.

Our *posiolok*, Shalashynsk, consisted of small shacks in the forest.

Our *posiolok* consisted of several dirty barracks.

We lived in barracks deep in the forest.

The barracks were set in a beautiful, huge forest.

Our barracks was located in the middle of the forest, seven kilometers from the *posiolok*. To get bread you had to walk to the *posiolok*, across a river.

Our *posiolok* was two hundred kilometers away from the White Sea.

Our *posiolok* was two thousand kilometers away from Vladivostok and was called "International." Winter lasts ten months there, and you could only get to the place during the two months of summer. The commandant said, "No one is ever released from this camp because there's no way back."

We were put in barracks, thirty people in each.

We were housed in barracks, with fifty people in each one.

We were housed eighty people to a barracks.

We lived a hundred people to a barracks.

We lived in barracks, two hundred people in each.

Two thousand people lived in five barracks.

At first we slept on the floor. Everyone had to build their own plank bed.

We slept out in the open before we built our barracks and plank beds.

We slept on the floor and woke up panic-stricken in the night, with mice the size of cats jumping all over us. We chased them away but they weren't afraid of us at all. When we complained to the commandant, he said, "In Russia you can get used to anything."

We slept in rotted-through tents. It poured rain and all our things rotted.

"Either you'll get used to it or you'll croak," the supervisors would tell us.

The barracks had no windowpanes.

The barracks floors had holes cut through them, which had served as toilets for previous prisoners.

In the barracks we were greeted by mosquitoes, ants, and other insects I didn't know.

The barracks were full of bedbugs that did not let us sleep.

The barracks were cramped and dirty. The bedbugs, lice and mice wouldn't leave us alone.

The barracks were filthy. Bedbugs and other insects plagued us day and night.

We lived in a barracks full of bedbugs and the gnats bit us viciously.

We were lying almost one on top of the other in those rotten barracks. The bedbugs bit us even when we slept outside, and their bites left pits in our flesh.

We were tormented by gnats, bedbugs, and fleas. At night we chased them with burning torches.

The barracks were dirty and cramped, and we were bitten by gnats, bedbugs, and lice. We chased the mice in the night but they weren't afraid of us at all.

The bedbugs were enormous, and they didn't even run away from us. People announced that they wouldn't go to work if they couldn't sleep at night. Iron beds were brought in, but even so we had to keep little lamps burning all night. When we ran out of kerosene and wicks, we burned pine torches.

The barracks were crawling with bedbugs and sleeping was out of the question. We decided to strike until they moved us to other housing. The NKVD arrested the strike leaders and divided us up between different *posiolki*.

We lived in mud houses among semisavage people who ate the raw flesh of animals they caught in the forest, as well as bark from trees. We ran to the Komi savages, begged meat from them, and ate it raw as they did. They advised us to eat tree bark. We dried it and pounded it with a stone, and Mama made dumplings with it. People said there were cannibals in the forest, and when we went berry picking we saw human bones.

There were 360 people living in the barracks, mostly Jews.

There were three hundred of us, but only six Polish families.

In our group there were 360 Jews.

Our group consisted of six hundred people, almost all Jews and very few Poles.

In our convoy there were a thousand people, all Jews.

In our *posiolok* there were five hundred Jews and one Pole.

In our *posiolok* there were a thousand Jews and Poles.

In our *posiolok* there were several thousand Poles and Jews.

There were six thousand of us, Jews and Poles. Mostly Jews.

In our transport there were many Poles. They were afraid of being exiled further away to more dangerous parts, so they pretended to be Jews.*

In our group there were Poles and Jews, who were always quarreling with each other.

In our *posiolok* there were thirty Poles for six hundred Jews, and relations with them were very good. Among them was a high Polish official—a devout Catholic and an anti-semite—who became friendly with my father. They would have long conversations and became convinced that religion was the only consolation in that terrible situation.

In the *posiolok* were many Poles who were friendly to us, helped us settle in, and gave us useful advice. The commandant, a Russian who hated Poles, would insult them and repeat every day that there would never be a Poland again and that they would stay in Russia forever.

---

*Polish gentiles erroneously believed that Jews were given preferential treatment in the Soviet Union.

In the *posiolok* were Poles who had been exiled earlier. They said they would not let any Jews in and we were sent back to Shevtera. It was pouring rain and we traveled all night, completely drenched. The next day mothers and children were taken by cart to *posiolok* Zhuravi. The road led through a river. While crossing it several carts tipped over and many children fell into the water. Leib Cywiak from Różan rushed to the rescue but he could not save them all.

We lived in barracks with Poles and Byelorussians, and we suffered a lot, particularly from the Byelorussians. We were insulted and humiliated and sometimes even beaten. The Jews asked many times for separate barracks, but our pleas were all in vain.

In *posiolok* number 54 we were housed with Ukrainians, who took everything we had, informed on us, and frequently beat us. We were 120 families among several hundred Ukrainians and our situation was intolerable.

In our *posiolok* there were exiled Russians who persecuted us terribly and said that we would never know freedom again.

The Russians were no better off than we were. They worked in the forest, went hungry, wore rags, and said that no one ever returned from exile.

The Russian exiles sentenced for counterrevolutionary activities assured us we would never leave Siberia.

The Russian exiles would torment us, saying we would never go back home and would all die there.

Exiled kulaks[*] lived in neighboring *kolkhozes*. They had their own cattle and poultry. They demanded five rubles for rotten potatoes and forty for a glass of milk but were happy to take clothes in barter. They were looking forward to war in order to escape but assured us that we would never leave Siberia and that this would be our grave.

In our *posiolok* we had Baruch Wajnman from Rozwadów and his wife, Shlomo Gusbojm from Krasna, Mr. Mansztajn, Mr. Haber, and Mr. Fajt.

In our barracks we had the Rozenfelds from Brest, the

[*]Rich peasants having their own resources and employing the labor of others.

Filars from Różan, the Krankenbergs from Wyszków, and Widow Morgensztern from Długosiodło with two children.

The commandant warned us that anyone who didn't work had no right to live.

❀

We Worked

Most deportees worked to exhaustion as woodcutters under slave-labor conditions, ravaged by hunger, cold, and disease. The mortality rate was enormous, especially among the children. Many surviving children were orphaned during this period, which lasted about one year.

We worked in the forest sawing and floating logs. Several people were killed by falling tree trunks in the first few days alone.

We worked in the forest twelve hours a day. During that time we had to saw three cubic meters of timber. Anyone who didn't make the quota went hungry. A tree crushed my father's arm—it was a miracle he survived the accident. During the time he was out sick, which lasted six weeks, he only got a half-ration of bread.

We worked in the forest, we built barracks, and got no pay for our work. My father could scarcely stand on his feet. The older people were dropping like flies.

On the first day an eighty-year-old Jew from Włodawa died chopping timber. Small children worked too.

We all worked in the forest, even Mama. The men cut down the trees, the women loaded the freight cars. We worked from dawn until nightfall. For our work we got a little bread and a few kopecks. Children were allowed to leave the *posiolok*, so we sold our old things to the Russian exiles and the local people, and that is what we lived off.

We worked felling timber. If you were late for work, they docked a quarter of your wages for three months. If you were late three times, they put you in jail for three months. No one in our family could make the quota, and we lived off food sent to us from Lwów.

We worked felling timber and loading freight cars. Small children stripped bark, because anyone who didn't work got no bread. Many people were killed by falling trees; others died from diseases. We sold all our things for food and were constantly hungry.

My father worked as a woodcutter and we helped him by sawing the timber into smaller pieces. We got one ruble and twenty kopecks for six cubic meters. In the summer we found blueberries, raspberries, and mushrooms in the forest. But summer is very short in Siberia.

The forest was completely wild and we had to remove bushes and weeds before we could get to the trees. This cut our arms and legs, and whenever we tore out roots, strange worms and insects would jump out and bite and sting us. People screamed that they wanted to go home. The NKVD men answered that they would send us back home once we had chopped down the whole forest.

My father, mother, and older sister worked in the forest. The forest was boggy and the gnats bit so badly that they'd come back from work with swollen faces.

When we worked we covered our faces with nets, which we all had to make for ourselves, but even so, we would come home with swollen faces.

My father and mother worked sawing timber. My father's legs swelled up and his hands got frostbite, but the commandant refused to release him from work. When Mama became weak she was allowed to chop branches.

In our family my father, mother, and oldest brother worked. My father was never able to make the quota.

My mother went to the forest and got seventy kopecks for cutting off branches. We could not live on that.

My father worked in the forest and earned eighty kopecks a day. I and my six-year-old brother worked too, and we were always hungry.

Everyone from ages sixteen to fifty-five had to work. I was twelve years old but I still reported for work, because what my father and the rest of the family earned was not enough. We sold our things to survive.

My quota was eight cubic meters a day but I could never saw more than one. Children up to the age of sixteen got four hundred grams of bread a day, and grown-ups who made their quotas got eight hundred. We worked from eight in the morning to eight at night. Sometimes the brigade leader would wake us up in the middle of the night to load the freight cars.

Children did not saw logs; instead we cleared the ground of roots. The quota was sixty roots a day, and we had to walk ten kilometers from the *posiolok* to where we worked. I was twelve years old and could not make the quota. If you made the quota you got eight hundred grams of bread, if you didn't you got only six hundred. In addition to that they paid you a few kopecks with which you were allowed to buy soup. My parents and brothers worked, but their earnings were not enough to buy soup for us all. When the temperature dropped to sixty below, my mother and I were let off work, but then for bread we had to rely on what my father and brothers made, while soup was out of the question.

I was twelve years old and my job was to strip tree bark, which old Russians made into shoes for the winter. They wore them over foot bindings to prevent blisters and as protection from the cold.

The older children stripped bark from trees and the younger ones gathered blueberries and mushrooms. The office paid a ruble for a kilo of blueberries and two for a kilo of mushrooms.

Our job was to burn twigs in the forest. The requirement was one hectare a day, but we could never manage more than one hectare a week because we were given only one box of matches a day and the damp twigs would not catch fire.

As a nine-year-old I went to work and made a few kopecks transporting timber. My warm pants soon wore out and I had nothing to put on. I got frostbite on my hands and feet.

Everyone had to work, even my youngest brother. The work was hard and I could never make the quota. We got four hundred grams of bread a day, while soup we had to buy from

the money we earned—which was not enough—and many
people died of starvation. We felt our strength draining away
and we didn't think we would ever be free again.

My father worked as a porter in the warehouses for fifty
kopecks a day. Seeing we could not live on that, he told the
commandant, Karchenko, that he would make him a pair of
boots in return for permission to open a shoemaker's workshop. After that my father earned good money, in addition to
which we got bread coupons. Everyone envied us.

My father said he was a shoemaker and got work in his
trade, while Mama and the four of us worked gathering moss.
The commandant was satisfied with my father's work and
would bring him bread. We shared it with our neighbors in
the barracks and everyone liked us. The children were especially nice to us since they knew they could expect a piece of
bread.

My father had brought a few notions, ribbons and buttons,
with him, and we got potatoes and bread in exchange for
them.

My older brothers both worked in the sawmill, where they
earned thirty kopecks each, while Chaya, who was a corset-
maker, had brought a suitcase full of work materials with her,
and took orders from the wives of local officials, engineers, and
other important people.

My brother had brought a little bit of leather with him and
started working as a shoemaker, but his leather soon ran out
and he had to go and work in the forest, where he earned one
ruble a day. That was not enough for food, especially when my
sister-in-law had a baby.

We had brought forty kilos of whole-grain flour with us,
and my sister sent us money and packages from Iwa, so in the
beginning we were not too badly off, but most people were
starving.

I and my brothers—fifteen-year-old Moishe and ten-year-
old Yossele—cleared a patch of forest and planted potatoes. It

was hard work and our hands bled. We did have potatoes, but only enough for two weeks.

We cleared a patch of forest and planted potatoes, beets, cucumbers, and onions. We made hotbeds for the plants. We would work late into the night, but before anything sprouted we were sent 150 kilometers further away.

My father and mother worked building railway embankments, and I and my sister gathered mushrooms in the forest, but we had almost nothing to eat.

My sister worked in the quarries and earned 110 rubles a month, but we were always hungry.

My father worked in an iron mine. He earned sixty rubles a month.

My father was ordered to work in a coal mine, but every day he would pass out on the job, and he was taken to the hospital. The Russian nurses were very kind, and when we came to visit him they would take us to the kitchen and give us something to eat.

My father was taken to a brick factory and ordered to carry clay. The work turned out to be too hard for him and he was given a job as a cart driver, but my father did not know how to drive horses. They gave him a stick and told him to hit the horse, but my father refused to hit the animal, so they sent him back to the barracks and took away his bread ration.

Mama worked in a brick factory and received eight hundred grams of bread, while we children got four hundred grams each. We did the housework for her and tried to have a little warm soup for her when she came home. We used to sing, *"Golodno, kholodno, dom daleko."*[*]

My father was taken on as a carpenter in a big factory. The work was very hard and they were not given much to eat. Fortunately my grandfather sent us food from Tarnopol.

My father worked in a factory that made railway ties, but earned very little. Had it not been for the packages we got from Przemyśl we would have died of hunger.

---

[*] "Hungry and cold and far from home" (Rus.)

My father worked as a loader. My stepmother could not work because she had a small baby, and my brother and I were still too young. Had it not been for the packages my grandmother and aunt sent us from Słonim we would have died of hunger.

My father worked in the forest, and his hands and feet were frostbitten. He earned ten kopecks a day and we could not afford soup in the canteen. We sold our old things and sometimes got a package from my grandfather, who had accepted a Soviet passport and had been sent to the town of Stalin.

My father, mother, sister, and brother worked two hundred meters underground. My mother and sister loaded coal onto wheelbarrows and pushed them to the elevator. The workday lasted twelve hours. My father and brother got five rubles each, my mother and sister four. Grown-ups were given eight hundred grams of bread, children four hundred. If you were five minutes late, a quarter of your pay was docked. When the mine was flooded during the autumn rains and no one was working, they gave the workers only five hundred grams of bread. We got food packages from our relatives, and that saved us.

Although we all worked, we were practically starving. We were saved by my sister, who used to send us food packages from a village near Pinsk.

We lived on packages that relatives sent us.

We lived on packages my sister sent us from Warsaw.

It was only thanks to the packages my grandfather sent that we survived the long months of forced labor.

We were eight in our family, and everyone worked. Each grown-up earned eighty kopecks a day, but that would only buy a box of matches.

Workers got four hundred grams of bread a day, nonworkers two hundred fifty. The canteen sold soup for fifty kopecks, but none of us could afford it, and we just lived on bread.

Soup in the canteen cost two and a half rubles. We could not afford such a luxury, so we lived on plain bread and hot water.

The ration was four hundred grams of bread each, two hundred for children. The bread was like clay and was impossible to eat until it dried out.

We got five hundred grams of bread a day, but sometimes the bread wasn't even delivered.

We got four hundred grams of bread each. Soup in the canteen cost sixty kopecks and none of us could afford it.

Workers got a kilo of bread a day, nonworkers four hundred grams. The watery soup in the canteen cost two rubles. Throughout the whole of our stay in the *posiolok* we could never once afford it. I so much wanted to eat something cooked that when people bought soup I would ask them to leave me a drop in the bottom. After a few months we were moved to a different *posiolok* that had no canteen, and you had to walk two kilometers to get soup. I would go and fetch soup for other people, and for every portion I brought I got two spoonfuls. I would bring five, six portions a day, but one time my hands got frozen on the way. I could not move my fingers for several weeks, and after that was not allowed to go for soup.

Some of the exiles worked in the forest and some on the railway embankments. The thermometer went down to fifty below and no one had clothes that were warm enough.

We worked even when it was fifty below. There was no medicine to treat frostbite, and people's fingers, ears, and noses fell off.

People went to work in the dark and came back in the dark, because the day was short and you had to walk many kilometers. The worst thing was the walking. People had frostbitten hands, feet, noses, and ears. A young Russian woman doctor performed amputations.

For digging the canal, people got six hundred grams of bread a day and twelve rubles a month. Twenty-five percent of wages were docked for lateness. My father got sick with rheumatism. Many people died.

My father worked as a loader, and I and my sister cut twigs off logs, but we still couldn't buy soup. Many people got sick, many died.

In the beginning my father, mother, sister, and brother worked in the forest while I and my little brother did the household chores. Later my father, who was a leather stitcher, got work in his trade, and my sister got a job in a workshop, sewing for the military. But all of them together earned so little that we were constantly hungry. Many people got sick and died.

Typhus and dysentery were frequent guests in the *posiolok*.

The most widespread disease was the kind of scurvy where pieces of flesh would drop off.

Most people got sick with scurvy, dysentery, and pneumonia. Among the people we knew, Tauba Kronenberg from Wyszków and Menachem Yechiel Morgensztern from Długosiodło died. We buried them not far from the barracks.

A few children lost their ability to speak but were not sent to the hospital because only the seriously ill were taken.

In summer it was easier because children gathered mushrooms and blueberries, but in winter it was not possible to leave the barracks and many people died.

Many people died of starvation, particularly those who were alone and had no children to gather mushrooms and blueberries for them. Some people started a hunger strike, but the commandant paid no attention to it. We tried in vain to persuade the strikers to eat our blueberries. When half of them died, the commandant promised to increase the bread rations.

The forest where my father worked was many kilometers away, and we could not sleep at night because of the gnats. Since supervision was not tight, we escaped to the village of Semyonovka. There my father worked in the fields and earned three hundred rubles a month, but there was not enough bread and we were still hungry. Once a week you could get dried peas in the cooperative.

The men were sent in a cart thirty-five kilometers away to fell timber. The gnats bit so terribly that people swelled up. The women rebelled and demanded that we be taken somewhere else. We were sent to Chet, where we had to build our own huts out of branches, since there was no wood for boards. Naturally, they were no protection against the rain. What struck us immediately was an enormous cemetery where thousands of Trotskyites were buried.

Forest work was very hard and we worked twelve- to fourteen-hour days, even in the freezing cold. Finally, people lost their patience and called a strike. A large group of NKVD men arrived. Twenty people were taken away in handcuffs and several families were sent to another *posiolok*. Our only achievement was that they opened a canteen.

One time a tree trunk fell on my father's leg. He lay in the barracks for weeks without any medical assistance. His leg became more and more swollen and we asked them to take him to the hospital, but our pleading was in vain. My older sister Zlata told them that if they did not take our father to the hospital we would not go to work, even at gunpoint. For two days we did not go to work and got nothing to eat. The commandant threatened us with harsh punishment, but we would not be intimidated, and on the third day my father was taken to the hospital. He was there for six months and in vain we pleaded with the commandant to allow us to visit him. He said, "That's what you get for striking." After our family struck, others began to follow suit. Anyone with any kind of complaint went on strike, and the commandant suspected that the organizer of these strikes was my sister Zlata. One night she was woken up and put in a little shack full of insects and mice. She was kept there every night and in the daytime sent out to work in the forest, where they counted only a quarter of her output. After two months she caught typhus and only then was allowed to return to the barracks. We all got infected from her but they refused to take us to the hospital. We recovered, but Mama started to spit blood.

Malaria was rampant in the camp. The gnats and bedbugs in our tents would not let us alone and people were going crazy. The grown-ups got a kilo of bread a day, and children got four hundred grams, but you could use that bread to plug holes, because it was like clay. One day thirty children died, and we thought that none of us would survive. The women and children organized a demonstration. The NKVD scattered the demonstrators and the grown-ups fled, but the children were not afraid. They arrested me, Itzhak Haber, Chaim Zylber, Naftali Rozenberg, and Zonensztern. The NKVD asked us what we wanted. We said, "We want to go back home because children are dying here." We were locked in the punishment cell, which was cold and dark, and we were given nothing to eat. Then we and a thousand others were sent to Shalashinsk, Sverdlovsk *oblast,* where the camp commandant was an exiled German and a terrible antisemite. There we chopped up tree stumps for steam-engine fuel. Children worked too. You earned forty kopecks a day, with which you could buy half a kilo of bread. In the neighboring village people earned five rubles loading freight cars. We went there but were not allowed to work. The commandant summoned everyone and made a speech, shouting, "There's enough land to bury you here, you Jewish swindlers." Then someone asked, "Are Kaganovich and other Jews in the government swindlers too?"[*] The commandant was removed immediately.

In Sosva there were Jews among the NKVD men, some of whom even spoke Yiddish. We sold them our watches and bought food with the money. Five thousand people worked in the sawmill and carpentry workshops. The manager-in-chief was a converted Jew called Goldberg. The pay was good, especially for making munitions boxes. We earned two hundred rubles a month, and a kilo of bread cost a ruble. We bought nourishing soup in the canteen. Apart from that everyone got half a *morga* of land.[†] We planted potatoes, onions, and sunflowers, and gathered redberries and blueberries in the forest. We built several nice, large barracks and painted them blue and white as a sign that we remembered Palestine.

The exiles themselves built a barracks out of felled timber, for a school. Two teachers arrived, Russian women who knew

---

[*]Lazar M. Kaganovich: Soviet deputy prime minister and high Party official.
[†]*Morga:* about 1.4 acres.

German and Polish. They had a lot of patience and helped the children study. We were very fond of them. The religious Jews tried to open a *kheyder* but the NKVD would not allow it.

❧

"Religious Criminals"

My father passed himself off as a cook. This was a very good trade, because anyone who had anything to do with the kitchen would bring home food. But you had to work Saturdays, so when Saturday came my father quit the job and we had to go hungry.

My parents would not work Saturdays. My father said, "God will not let us die of hunger for keeping the Sabbath." And sure enough, we started getting packages and money from relatives in western Galicia, and later when the packages stopped coming we sold some of our things. On Saturdays my father would teach us Talmud, because his greatest concern was that we should grow up to be devout Jews.

My father would not work Saturdays for anything and would use his last kopecks to hire replacements in order not to break the holy day.

The commandant of the *posiolok* would threaten my father that he would never be released from exile, but my father paid no attention and refused to work Saturdays.

My father did not go to work on Saturdays. They threatened him with prison, but when that didn't work they left him alone.

My grandfather organized services on Friday evenings. The commandant harassed him for his religious activities but my grandfather ignored it.

They called my father and the *shoykhet* "dirty priests." They interrogated them and accused them of making people take Saturdays off. Every Saturday was interrogation day, but in the end those who did not want to work on Saturdays did not work.

My father would not work Saturdays. The commandant drew up a report and told him to sign it. My father refused to sign and was put in the punishment cell, which was dark and damp, and was given nothing to eat. When he was let out he still would not work Saturdays, and the commandant pretended not to notice.

My brother Abraham-Jakub would not work Saturdays. They sent him for three months to a penal camp where he was only given a half-ration of bread, but there too he refused to work Saturdays. Finally, seeing they were getting nowhere with him, the Bolsheviks left him alone.

My father would not work Saturdays, but they put him in the punishment cell several times and he had to give in.

On Saturdays my father would take his *tallis* and prayer book with him to the forest.

We were forced to go to school on Saturdays. I would not break the holy day for anything in the world and did not go to school on Saturdays. They arrested my mother. They said they were not arresting my father because that would be a waste of manpower, but they did arrest many other mothers.

I did not want to go to a Soviet school, so I did not do my homework and pretended to be stupid. When punishment didn't work they threw me out of the school.

I went to school, and when I got home my grandfather taught me Torah so that I should not forget I was a Jew. My grandfather would also gather children from neighboring barracks and tell us the history of the Jews.

There was a Jew in our *posiolok* who prayed every day and would not work Saturdays. They arrested him and took away all his things, even his wedding ring. His wife and children were not given bread, and one child died of starvation. The whole family would have died had we not brought them some blueberries and mushrooms, which we gathered in the forest.

With Rosh Hashana approaching, my father worried about finding a shofar. After a while we found out that in a *posiolok*

forty kilometers away there was a young man who used to make shofars in Poland. We collected money in our *posiolok* and the neighboring one, and within a few weeks he made eight shofars, one of which came our way.

Before the holidays the commandant called in my grandfather and warned him that he would be severely punished if he organized services.

Before the High Holidays the commandant called in my father and told him that if he wanted to pray he should pray by himself. He added that Stalin's constitution, while not prohibiting religious worship, did not permit religious propaganda. Moreover, assembling in large groups was prohibited in the *posiolok*. My father answered that he was not going to make propaganda with anyone but could not guarantee that people would not come to him for holiday prayers of their own free will, if they felt the need.

The efforts of my father and Rabbi Hurwicz from Nowy Sącz to be released from work on Rosh Hashana were unsuccessful. They were merely promised that the older people would be released on Yom Kippur, and only on condition that they would not pray together. Naturally, people *did* pray together, and in the middle of the day our barracks was surrounded by the NKVD. My father and Rabbi Hurwicz were sent off to town, to jail, where they were beaten for six weeks and given only bread and water. They appointed a Jewish attorney for the trial since the defendants did not know Russian. The defense counsel explained to the court the meaning of the Yom Kippur holiday, especially for rabbis and for old people who had a hard time giving up generations-old traditions. The court acquitted them both and the informer was punished by God—killed at work by a falling log.

On Rosh Hashana morning everyone was praying. We had no Torah but we did find a shofar. The commandant burst in with militiamen, dispersed the congregation, and took my father off to his office. They accused him of work sabotage, for which he could have gotten several years in prison, but they just sentenced him to a salary reduction of 25 percent.

On Rosh Hashana everyone showed up for prayers.

Among the exiles was a cantor who sang so beautifully that non-Jews from nearby barracks would flock to hear him. At the most solemn moment, the commandant burst into the barracks and shouted, "None of you will get out of here alive anyway, so there's no point praying!" On Yom Kippur no one went to work. The commandant screamed and threatened but did not carry out any of his threats.

On the first day of the holidays thirty people gathered in our barracks. In the middle of a prayer five NKVD men burst in with the commandant. They arrested my father, the *shoykhet,* and another elderly Jew with a beard. They led them through the *posiolok* like criminals, dragging my father by the collar. The way they arrested my father during prayers and treated him like a criminal made such an impression on the Jews that the next day everyone, even the freethinkers, left the job and came to our barracks for prayers. Their names were taken, and a few dozen were put in punishment cells, but before Yom Kippur the commandant came to my father and said that because of the religious enthusiasm he had seen among the exiles he was releasing everyone from work for that day.

During the holidays thirty Jews did not show up for work. The commissar carried out an inspection and caught the ones who were leading the services. The rest he dispersed, threatening harsh punishment. Despite this, people assembled again to complete the service. The next day my father was sentenced to six weeks' detention, while the others had their pay cut for six months. Yet on Yom Kippur none of the Jews in our *posiolok* went to work, regardless of the penalties. From then on the commissar would release Jews from work on holidays.

On Rosh Hashana there were no services, but on Yom Kippur no one paid attention to the threats, and communal prayers with a cantor were organized in our barracks. The commandant came in but no one budged. The commandant threatened to prosecute my grandfather, but the prayers were not interrupted.

On the first day of Rosh Hashana no one went to work. The NKVD men arrived and began looking for the organizers of the sabotage. They threatened such terrible punishment that the next day everyone went to work. On Yom Kippur people fasted and said prayers while working.

The Jews asked to be released from work on Yom Kippur. The commandant replied that anyone who rebelled would be sent to Siberia, so everyone worked. But in the evening prayers were said in our house.

We decided to take off Yom Kippur without asking our bosses, because we knew in advance they would not release us. In the morning the commandant came and asked why we were not going to work. We said we were observing the Day of Atonement. The commandant became angry and brought in NKVD men. Moniek Ajmer from Rozwadów explained the meaning of the holiday to them in Russian. After a brief discussion, the NKVD men answered that Russia did not recognize that kind of holiday and that if we did not go to work we would go to jail for sabotage. Moniek Ajmer, speaking on our behalf, said we were prepared for sacrifices. He was taken to Sverdlovsk along with several others who were considered to be the organizers. Three months later they returned and told us they had met a rabbi in prison who had been tortured to make him reveal where in Russia there were other rabbis and *shoykhets*.

On Yom Kippur my father held services in our barracks. NKVD men burst in, arrested him, and put him down on record as being a religious criminal. My father's brother, Rabbi Joel Frenkiel, was also branded a religious criminal, and both had to endure NKVD harassment.

We decided not to work on Yom Kippur, and everyone gathered together for prayers. NKVD men arrived and threatened to prosecute us but we did not interrupt the service. The next day I was taken to court along with the grown-ups. Everyone had 25 percent of their wages deducted, but I was not punished since I was underage.

The Jews decided not to go to work on Yom Kippur and to spend the day in prayer. The commandant got the NKVD, and they were about to arrest us, but then they received a delegation from our group and the matter was settled amicably.

It cost us three suits of clothes for the NKVD men and one for the commandant.

Our family was among the best workers in the mine, and we were entitled to buy newspapers and movie tickets. We missed only one day of work—Yom Kippur. My father said he would never allow us to work on that day. The commandant said that because we worked honestly he would not accuse us of sabotage.

The commandant said he would not allow us to put up *sukkas* for the holidays because he feared a fire, but my father ignored the ban and did put up a *sukka*.

In the middle of winter they took my father's books away. They accused him of spending too much time with them and also of teaching children. The commandant wanted to burn the books, but my father petitioned the NKVD and received the reply that they would not be burned but would be taken away and stored.

For Passover my sister sent us thirty kilos of matzo, raisins for wine, and chicken fat.

For Passover we got from Byelorussia matzo, chicken fat, raisins for wine, and even holiday dishes. And my father organized matzo baking for the neighboring *posiolki*.

My brother from Grodno sent us matzo for Passover.

We had no matzo for Passover, and my father fasted because he would not eat bread.

In our *posiolok* there was an observant Jew who held services in his barracks, like in a synagogue. One day NKVD men showed up. He was sentenced to four months' imprisonment. The man's wife, who had three small children, could not go to work, and they stopped her bread ration. Had it not been for the packages from her relatives, she would have died of starvation. The commandant, furious that she somehow managed stay alive despite everything, accused her of speculation in foodstuffs. She was arrested and her children were left all alone, so my mother took them into our barracks and told my father, "We'll just pretend we have three more."

The Jews in our *posiolok* would not work on Saturdays, and the commandant threatened that anyone who did not work on Saturday would get no bread for the rest of the week. That didn't scare anyone, and on Saturday no one went to work. The commandant withheld the bread and prohibited the canteen from selling us soup. After a few days, when people started to faint from hunger, the young men rebelled and beat up the commandant. The commandant called in the NKVD and they decided to transfer all the Jews to a penal *posiolok*. We were sent to Asino, and from there we traveled ten days by train to a *posiolok* that had gold and copper mines. We were carefully watched to make sure we did not talk to the Russian exiles, who went around in rags.

My father prayed every day together with other Jews. The commandant threatened that if he found them praying once more, he would put them in jail. This set off a rebellion among the observant Jews. The NKVD arrested and deported several of them to another area. That roused people up even more. The graves of the Trotskyites near the barracks were a hint of what we could expect, so we made contact with two other camps to prepare a joint escape. In our *posiolok* there were 150 Poles, who did not interfere in our business, but since we did not trust them we did not let them in on our plans. We secretly made several hundred handcarts. We cut the wheels from a tree trunk. The Poles did not participate but did not give us away. On the Soviet holiday, when the commandant and his deputy got drunk, people loaded their things onto the carts, the women tied their children onto their backs, and in the night twelve thousand people set off along forest paths to the river. We had gone about twenty kilometers when NKVD men on horses intercepted us. Their leader advised us to go back. He promised better working conditions and more food, but the crowd did not move. The women were particularly obstinate. The NKVD arrested twenty men but it didn't help. When a large cargo boat arrived, fifteen hundred people forced their way on board, chased the sailors off, and sailed away toward Tomsk. Six planes flew over and fired shots to scare us. Artillery guns were also brought in, but the exiles said they weren't afraid, and better death than such a life. The NKVD negotiated with threats and promises. After four days our supplies ran out and we had nothing to eat, so we returned to Asino. They treated us better: we got potatoes and noodles, and even people who could not work got food. That lasted for six weeks, and then it got worse again. We planned another rebellion and escape, but the NKVD, noticing that something was going on, liquidated the camp and sent us off in different directions. Our group of fifteen hundred people was sent to Sosva, in Sverdlovsk *oblast*.

One day everyone left the job and went to the river. The NKVD wanted us to turn back, but the exiles threatened them with saws and axes. The NKVD men fired warning shots. "We'd rather die than live like this!" the exiles shouted. A plane flew over and dropped leaflets promising that we would be moved to another *posiolok* with much better conditions. When we did go back they arrested several Jews, and on the third day a bolt of lightning killed a woman in the forest. At her funeral the exiles vowed they would not return to work. For two days no one worked, and the authorities didn't react. Then the order came, and we were moved to Kamensk in Sverdlovsk *oblast*. In the new *posiolok* workers got a kilo of bread a day, nonworkers half a kilo. In the canteen you could buy nutritious soup for thirty kopecks. My mother sold our things for food. A few months later, when the order came to leave the *posiolok*, no one wanted to budge, but Russian exiles who had been sent to take our places chased us out and beat those who resisted. The *posiolok* we were sent to next was near Syktyvkar.

At the funeral of the Jewish woman killed by lightning, Rabbi Frenkiel of Kraków said that everyone should vow not to go to work anymore. The next day no one worked, and we packed our bundles to flee, not caring where we went. In the afternoon a detachment of NKVD men from Novosibirsk appeared and started firing into the air. They arrested the leaders of the rebellion, and our situation got even worse.

When the lightning bolt killed the woman from Zamość, nobody believed we would get out of there alive, and we decided to escape. We traveled in little boats we built ourselves, but NKVD motorboats stopped us. We were marched to a *posiolok* in a wasteland where we had polar bears as visitors. We begged for a different place and were sent to the Urals for the hay-making. There we each earned twenty kopecks a day, but they didn't pay us even that ridiculous sum, and we were getting swollen from hunger and gnat bites. When the hay-making was over they sent us to *posiolok* Sashla in Sverdlovsk *oblast*, where we had to work even when it was sixty below.

The cold was terrible, and the snow reached up to the grown-ups' necks. During blizzards we were afraid the snow would bury us in our barracks.

We slept in wooden barracks, and all night long the person on duty kept putting logs on the fire. We slept in our clothes, and my mother wrapped me up in rags as best she could, but when I woke up I would break off pieces of ice from my ears.

It was very cold and sad. Mama became sick and died. She was so young, only thirty-one. We four orphans were left behind. My father was dropping from exhaustion. As a woodcutter he earned twenty rubles a month, and we would have died of hunger had we not sold Mama's things.

Mama caught cold and was in bed with a high fever for eight days before a doctor showed up. He said it was pneumonia and gave her a note for the hospital. My father tried to get a cart but the commandant said all the horses were needed for work until Sunday. My father cried and repeated that Mama would not last until Sunday, but the commandant said that in Russia work was the most important thing and it could not be disrupted because of one person. The fever worsened, Mama got weaker and weaker, and on Saturday morning she died. She was buried in the forest among the other exiles.

Mama caught pneumonia. My father and older brother had to go to work, so I became her nurse. There was no doctor in

the *posiolok*. After much begging I got permission to bring in
a medical attendant from the neighboring *posiolok*. He said
her condition was critical. I begged him to have her taken to
the hospital. He answered that there was no room in the hospital and told us to put cupping glasses on her. I had no cupping glasses, only three regular glasses we had brought from
Białystok, and instead of alcohol I used kerosene. Her condition steadily worsened. I found out that twenty kilometers
from our *posiolok* there was a hospital with Polish doctors. I
got a pass from the commandant and went. I described
Mama's condition to a Polish doctor, and he gave me a note
for her to be admitted to the hospital. I ran to the commandant with the note. Only when I broke down in sobs did he
allow me to take a horse, because in Russia a horse is more
important than a human being. The next morning I harnessed
the horse, and the children helped me carry Mama onto the
cart, because my father and brother were in the forest. After a
few kilometers, Mama died in the cart and I turned back to the
posiolok. We buried her by a tree, on which we carved an
inscription.

Mama caught a chill and was taken to the hospital, but her
condition did not improve because they paid no attention to
the patients. One day she felt so bad that she asked my father
to bring us to her. He had to wait for us to come back from
work in the forest, and when we arrived at the hospital Mama
was already dead. When we were about to take her away, the
hospital director said her body was to be cut up because the
young doctors had to learn. My father said if they did that he
would kill himself and us. He ran from one doctor to another
all day, while I and my brother guarded Mama and cried
because we were afraid they would cut her up. In the evening
my father obtained a note with permission to bury her. We
guarded her all night, and in the morning took her by cart to
the *posiolok*. Our father dug with a shovel, and we used bare
hands. No one helped us, for everybody was at work. In the
evening ten Jews came after work, and my brother said *kaddish* with them.

Mama got brain fever from worry, and there was no medical assistance. When she died, my father gathered ten Jews and started to say *kaddish*. For that crime he and my two brothers were put in the punishment cell.

My father and mother came down with dysentery. We sold our last shirts, hired a cart, and drove them to the hospital, but they refused to admit them. Our pleas were in vain, so we drove them back, seriously ill. They were in bed for two weeks in the barracks and their condition grew worse every day. Finally the commandant himself took pity and drove them to the hospital, but by then it was too late. My father died on Saturday and my mother four days later. I was the sole support and guardian of my little sisters. I could not keep them with what I earned, and since there was nothing more to sell, the three of us went hungry. The commandant went into town and obtained permission to send us to our grandparents, who were in a *posiolok* near Novosibirsk.

My older sister worked clearing snow from roads, but the commandant thought that the quota for women was too low and introduced a piecework system—the less work you did, the smaller your bread ration. After working under this system, my sister came back to the barracks sick, and two days later died of pneumonia. Each day several people died.

Uncle Itzhak and his son were with us. His wife had remained under German occupation. Both got sick with typhus. They were not admitted to the hospital, and there was no doctor in the *posiolok*. They lay sick in our barracks, and my uncle died. I cried a lot at his funeral. He was buried in the forest along with several other Jews, for people were dying every day.

When my two brothers, six-year-old Hersh and five-year-old Itzhak, came down with measles, the commandant would not allow them to stay in the barracks and ordered them to be taken to the hospital. My mother begged that they be allowed to stay, for fear that they might catch cold on the way, but to no avail. They were wrapped in blankets and taken by sledge. They did catch cold, and died three days later. My father was afraid an autopsy would be done on them and spent the whole day in the hospital until they gave him the bodies.

With the help of my older brother, my father dug a grave and buried them together. Then my father got sick and remained in bed for six weeks. We sold our things to stay alive. We were moved to the worst barracks, where even during the day mice scampered all over the bed, pestering my sick father, so that I had to chase them away with a stick.

My father was a healthy man. I don't recall him being sick before the war. At first he felt just fine and worked like everyone else. One day he felt weak at work, but the supervisor said he would be all right. He died in the forest before everyone's eyes. His body was brought back in the evening after work. All night long we and Mama stayed by him and chased the mice away. At dawn we sewed a garment for him from a couple of shirts and wrote his first name, last name, and the date on a board.

At first we would sell clothes and receive parcels from relatives in Byelorussia. Then we had nothing more to sell and the parcels stopped coming, and we all got sick with a terrible disease called scurvy. Our blood turned to pus, our bodies looked like open wounds, and our flesh came off in pieces.

Mama sold everything we had, but we still could not afford to buy soup. My older brother Moishe was unable to work because his hands and feet were frostbitten and he was covered in sores. There was nothing to treat them with. Grandfather fell ill with dysentery, but they would not admit him to the hospital because he was too old, and after a few days he died. We buried him in the forest and Moishe carved his name on a tree so we could visit his grave. We missed Grandfather a lot because whenever we had had hunger pangs he would tell us stories about himself and our father, and we would forget our hunger.

My brother Hersh fell ill, and we didn't know what it was. Since there was no medical help he died after a few weeks and we buried him in the middle of the forest.

My youngest brother got sick with measles. There was no doctor or medicine and the little thing died.

Many people died of hunger, particularly young children.

After work my father performed the duties of rabbi and

grave digger and with the help of a few other Jews buried the dead. And so a cemetery came into being, which we enclosed with a wooden fence.

The commandant did not care about the high mortality rate. He said, "All exiles must die in Siberia."

When the News of the Amnesty Came

On June 22, 1941, despite the mutual nonaggression pact, Nazi Germany attacked the Soviet Union. Its forces made a quick advance to the east. In the wake of this attack, on July 30 an agreement was signed in London between the Polish prime minister-in-exile, General Władysław Sikorski, and the Soviet ambassador in London, Valerii Mayski, in the presence of Winston Churchill and British foreign minister Anthony Eden. The agreement called for a resumption of diplomatic relations between Poland and the Soviet Union and cooperation in the war against Germany. A Polish army was established on Soviet soil. It was headed by General Władysław Anders, who was released for this purpose from Moscow's Lubianka prison, and it was known as the Anders army. In addition, an amnesty was to be granted to Soviet-imprisoned Polish citizens.

When the German–Soviet war broke out we had to work two hours longer and we got less bread.

When the war broke out we worked twelve hours a day. Bread rations were reduced to six hundred grams for grown-ups and four hundred grams for children—and two days a week we worked without any pay, for the defense of the country.

When the war broke out the bread rations for workers were reduced to six hundred grams and the workday increased to fourteen hours.

When the war broke out the NKVD men goaded people on without allowing them to catch their breath. My parents would come back from the mine half-dead and collapse from exhaustion.

When the war broke out they reduced our bread rations and everyone had to go to work, even my sick mother and me, though I was only eleven.

With the outbreak of war they reduced our bread rations and increased the work quotas. My father could hardly stand on his feet. Every day I went with him to work, to help him out.

After the war broke out we got only six hundred grams of bread, two hundred for the children, and we were facing starvation.

When the war broke out they increased the work hours, and there were days when we got no bread at all.

After the war broke out there was more work in the camp but less bread.

After the war with the Germans broke out a special meeting was convened where they called on us to "work strenuously for our common cause."

After the German–Russian war broke out the commandant convened a meeting and announced that we all had to work for our common cause.

After the German–Soviet war broke out a commission arrived with the head of the NKVD, who announced that we were now allies and had to work even more zealously for our common cause.

When the war broke out our boss accused us of being spies, and they watched every step we took.

When the war broke out they increased the workday by two hours and reduced the bread rations, and our parcels stopped coming.

When the war broke out we stopped getting parcels from my sister in Iwa.

Our situation got worse when the war broke out because we lost contact with Mama, our relatives sent us no more parcels, our bread rations were cut, and they pushed us to work without a break.

When the war broke out, not only were our bread rations reduced but we also stopped getting parcels from Poland, and we thought we would die of starvation.

When the war broke out the parcels stopped coming, our bread rations were reduced to two hundred grams, and we worked twelve hours a day. My father said he would not survive the work and the hunger.

When the war broke out my parents had to work fourteen hours a day and our parcels stopped coming. We thought we would all die—then the news of the amnesty arrived.

After the German–Russian war broke out our situation got so much worse that we thought we would never get out alive; then suddenly the news of the amnesty arrived.

That there was a war we learned one day from the guards, who asked us to keep it a secret. Then we understood why the bread rations had been reduced.

That there was a war we found out only after two weeks.

We knew nothing at all about the outbreak of war.

No one in the *posiolok* knew about the outbreak of war, and only after some time did we find out about the amnesty.

We were cut off from the world, but a parcel of flour, chicken fat, and other things that we received was wrapped up in newspapers. From those newspapers we found out about the Sikorski Agreement, and we showed them to our boss.

We found out about the agreement between Russia and Poland by chance: a Jew from Kiev sent us a parcel in which he had put a newspaper containing the news. The commandant had known about it for two months but had kept it secret from us. We went on strike. They threatened that if we did not go back to work we would get nothing to eat, but we insisted that we wanted to leave, so the strike dragged on. Two senior NKVD officials arrived, and they admitted that as Polish citizens we were entitled to leave, but they advised us to stay because the Germans were bombing trains. We answered that we wanted to leave anyway, to which they replied that it was the rainy season and the trucks could not take us over muddy roads. We said we would go on foot and lodge a complaint with the Polish consulate. Then the NKVD men changed their tune. They allowed us to take all our things and paid us all our back wages. We got bread for two days and tractors— which we had to push since the roads really were muddy. At the railway station they demanded 118 rubles a person for tickets, but none of us had that kind of money. "You brought us here without a ticket, so take us back without a ticket," we told them. They said we were disrupting traffic and wanted to throw us out of the station, but a Lieutenant Epstein from Kraków just happened to be there at the time, and he advised us to send a telegram complaining to the Polish mission in Buzuluk. Then the order came from Moscow to feed us and load us onto the train.

When the news of the amnesty came, our boss said it did not apply to Jews, only Poles.

When the amnesty was announced the commandant told us that it did not apply to Jews.

When the news of the amnesty came our boss announced that it applied to Poles, not Jews. Only when we appealed to the authorities in Sverdlovsk did we get our papers.

We reached the place the barges were leaving from, but we couldn't get onto any of them. We had to work for the NKVD men for two weeks to get a place on a barge. It then took us twenty-one days to sail to Omsk.

After the amnesty was announced my father was paid four months in back wages, and we traveled to Teguldet. There we had to wait out in the open for two weeks before we got on a barge to Asino.

People had been waiting weeks by the river because the NKVD refused to give them barges. Kornblit from Warsaw went to Tavda with a delegation and prevailed on them to give us a barge for our things, but we had to go to Tabory on foot. There we got a barge to Tavda and traveled for four days without any bread.

When our papers arrived we went by river to Tavda, starving on the way.

When the amnesty for Polish citizens was announced in August, we quit work that same day and went to Chelyabinsk, where we waited for a train to Tashkent.

At the news of the amnesty we quit work, even though the commandant was very angry.

When the amnesty was announced the commandant pressured us to stay, but everyone wanted to leave. We weren't working and we got no bread. A delegation went to the NKVD and a month later we got our papers.

When the news of the amnesty came they tried to hold on to us with the promise of potatoes, wood to build a house, and a cow for each family.

After the amnesty was announced for Polish citizens a senior NKVD official came and asked us to stay. He promised land, tools, and seeds and assured us that no one would take our Polish citizenship away. But nobody would listen to him.

After the amnesty was announced they asked us to stay and promised things would be better, but we did not want to, and we set off in the direction of Samarkand.

After the amnesty was announced the commandant tried to persuade my father to stay in the mine. He offered him better working conditions and pointed out that he would always be able to leave Russia with a Polish passport, but my father would not listen to him and we set off for Uzbekistan.

After the amnesty was announced NKVD men pointed out the advantages of staying and stressed how uncertain our future would be if we left. No one wanted to stay and they issued us affidavits, with which we set off for Ishym, where we met large numbers of Poles.

We found out about the amnesty toward the end of August. Senior NKVD officials arrived and pressured us to stay, and the commandant spoke of the difficulties and dangers of traveling south, particularly for families with young children. But very few remained.

After Yom Kippur we were informed of the amnesty for Polish citizens and received affidavits permitting us to travel to small towns. We were not allowed into large towns.

In October a car arrived in our *posiolok* and two officers got out, a Pole and a Russian. They informed us that we could go wherever we wanted, with the exception of large towns.

One day a Polish officer arrived, and we were told we could go wherever we wanted. We went on foot to the station, which was two days' walk from the *posiolok,* and there we found thousands of people.

After the amnesty was announced a Polish commission arrived. They delivered food and clothing, but only Poles got them. Jews were given nothing.

A commission came to us consisting of NKVD representatives and a few Polish officers, and they informed us that we were free and could go wherever we wanted. We said we wanted to go to Tashkent, because there you could get bread and oranges like in Palestine.

When the news came of the release of Polish citizens we decided to head for warmer parts, because we had no warm clothes.

When the news of the amnesty came we thought we were coming back to life, but our commandant went around looking sheepish.

It is hard to describe our joy when we found out about the amnesty. The Russian exiles envied us.

After many months we got news of the amnesty, but just as everyone was rejoicing, my father had a heart attack and died. We had a lot of difficulties with the funeral. My brother lost his mind because of it and was taken to an insane asylum. I carried my father to the cemetery by myself and buried him myself. Everyone had fled and I wanted to leave too, but I felt bad leaving my brother behind. I sold everything to save him, but he died after a few weeks. They refused to give me his body. I was sure they had poisoned him.

Everyone had left, but we remained behind with a group of Russian exiles because my father and uncle were considered to be religious criminals, so we were not given permission to leave. Only four weeks later did a senior official arrive from the NKVD, a Jew who was moved by our tears, and we received red papers—for criminals—with permission to travel to Revda.

After fourteen months of exile a commission arrived that gave us Polish passports, and we were released. We had no money for the journey and we walked three hundred kilometers to Tavda.

We hired a cart to Tavda and got on a train heading south.

It took us two weeks to get to Archangelsk, where we waited several days for a train.

When the announcement of the amnesty appeared we went to Revda. By then my father and sister were so weak that they could not work. My brother worked day and night in a brick factory but without pay. My father sold his coat and we got on a train for Tashkent.

After the amnesty was announced we traveled to Syktyvkar, but there was no bread or work there, so we set off in the direction of Samarkand.

When news arrived of the treaty between Poland and Russia we left for Kazakhstan.

After the amnesty was announced we traveled to Kazakhstan with my father, who had tuberculosis, because the doctors said that going south might save him.

After the amnesty was announced the *posiolok* was liquidated and we were moved into town, where after some time we got exit permits and waited many weeks for a train, during which period we sold what was left of our things.

Like the other Jews, Mama sold our last shirts, and we chipped in together to hire a train car.

It took several weeks for us to get a place on the train to Bukhara.

With our last shirts we bought tickets to Samarkand.

With a group of five families we hired a train car to Bukhara, for which we paid fifty-five rubles each.

My father hired a train car together with a family we knew and we set off in the direction of Bukhara.

When we found out about the amnesty we went to Turkestan.

The journey took five weeks. We paid enormous sums for food.

Our journey took six weeks. We got bread once every four days and we were constantly hungry.

When we got bread they would enter it in our papers. I would use a piece of bread to erase the date in order to get another ration.

It took us seven weeks to travel from Archangelsk to Bukhara.

The journey was very long. Whenever the train stopped my brother would bring cabbages and rutabagas from the fields.

We traveled hungry for a very long time. Whenever the train stopped, the children would run out into the fields and pull whatever they could out of the ground.

When the train stopped, we would pick grass from the fields, and that is what we lived on.

There were Poles on the train who had worked in the fields in Siberia and had brought along baskets of potatoes, while my brother had nothing. I felt terribly sorry watching his little baby with nothing to eat. Once at a station I saw some Russian soldiers eating bread. I got out and they gave me a piece to take back to my little nephew, but in the meantime the train had left. I cried bitterly, and the stationmaster asked the soldiers to take me to the station where the Polish convoys stopped. I did find my brother there, and he scolded me and told me never to get off the train again. But the hunger pangs were very bad and I would beg from soldiers at every station. Once I got a package of rusks, so the baby had something to suck on for a few days. Three times the train left without me and I found my brother again, but the fourth time I did not, and the stationmaster sent me to a *kolkhoz*.

We could get nothing to eat at any station, and we ate wild plants from the fields. Little Heniek came down with typhus and Mama had to get off the train with him, because people were afraid of getting infected, so we traveled on alone.

The journey lasted a long time. We ate wild plants, and many people got sick with dysentery.

Our journey to Tashkent took six weeks, and my father got sick on the way.

In Chelyabinsk they would not let us off the train. My father and sister got sick with typhus, and when we arrived in Chkalov they both died.

The journey was long and difficult and everyone was sick with dysentery.

The journey took two months. Several people in our group died.

Our journey took six weeks. Many people became sick and died from eating wild plants picked in the fields. They were buried in the fields.

It was a terrible journey. We would stop in stations for forty-eight hours and it was hard to find even a piece of bread. An epidemic broke out and all the children under four died.

Many people died on the way. They were taken off and laid in the stations, where no one paid any attention to them. We children were so afraid of the dead that we did not get out at the stations to look for food.

In Kizil-Tepe we unexpectedly met my Uncle Shimon on his way from Komi, where they had mistreated him terribly. He was twenty-eight but looked like an old man. He had eaten nothing but oil cakes and had a sick stomach. Our joy at finding him was short-lived because he soon came down with dysentery and died.

We journeyed for many weeks, hungry all the time, and when we arrived in Kattakurgan the town was full of refugees and we slept on the street. Many people died of hunger.

In Samarkand they would not let us into the town, and for two weeks we slept out in the open.

In Samarkand the railway station was besieged with people. We had nowhere to go and NKVD men chased us from one place to another.

In Samarkand we had nowhere to spend the night and we lay by the railway station, in the snow.

We arrived in Samarkand on a cold, rainy day. We spent the night in the mud on the street and were robbed of everything we had.

In Samarkand thousands of refugees were roaming the streets.

In Tashkent people were lying side by side on the street. Our sack of belongings was stolen. My father was very upset because his *tallis* was in that sack.

We arrived in Tashkent without my mother. We wandered through the streets and couldn't find anything to eat.

When we arrived in Bukhara thousands of people were camping out in the open, and prowling among them were

Uzbek thieves. Many seriously ill people were lying in the streets.

In Bukhara we spent our nights at the station because no one would take us in.

In Bukhara people lay on the street because, apart from us, refugees were pouring in from all the evacuated Soviet towns.

In Turkestan, which was full of refugees, we spent our nights on the street in the mud. People were dying of hunger.

In Kizil-Tepe we lived on the street. We were dying of hunger, so we went to Kizduban.

We arrived in Turkestan, which was full of refugees from towns occupied by the Germans.

We arrived in Kermine and wandered through the streets.

After two years of hard labor and hunger we didn't have the strength to stand on our feet. When we arrived in Tashkent they wouldn't let us off the train because of an epidemic in the town, which was full of refugees, and there was no space even on the streets.

We traveled from Tashkent to Samarkand, but there too we lived on the street, sleeping in the mud, and many times we wished we were dead.

In Samarkand we spent a whole week in the mud before we got a place in a stable.

In Bukhara my father managed to barter a watch for a place for us to sleep in a cellar. People were dying on the streets of hunger and disease.

After many nights spent in the fields we found room in a stable, but we had nothing to buy food with.

We arrived in Kurkurovsk, and after a few weeks of trudging around without a roof over our heads we got a stable to sleep in, but in vain did my father try to find work, and we ate grass that Mama cooked.

In Turkestan, after a long search, we found a mud hut, but we had nothing to buy bread with. Typhus spared no one, and many of our friends died.

In Samarkand we spent two weeks out in the open until my father found some hole for us to live in. We all got sick with typhus.

In Samarkand we lived on the street for three weeks. My father and mother got sick with typhus and my little sister and I took care of them.

In Tashkent Helenka, Irka, and I got sick and lay on the street with a fever before we were taken to the hospital. When we left the hospital we found our mother, but without little Heniek.

In Bukhara there were many Jews from Poland who were dying from the epidemic, and every day there were dozens of corpses lying on the street.

In Samarkand it was impossible to get bread, and many refugees were dying on the street.

Hundreds of people were lying on the streets, the sick with the healthy, the living with the dead. People robbed each other—and everyone was robbed by the Uzbeks, who were impossible to chase away. We children got so used to the sight of dead people that we stopped being afraid of them.

When we arrived in Bukhara a kilo of bread cost a ruble, a kilo of soybeans six rubles, and a kilo of prunes thirty. After three months the price of flour went up to a hundred rubles per kilo and bread was sold only with ration cards, only four hundred grams per person, and only to registered inhabitants.

In the beginning the Bukharan Jews helped us but eventually they could not deal with such destitution either.

We used to meet Bukharan Jews who knew Hebrew. They could not be of much help, since the rich ones had been exiled long ago and the poor had nothing to eat themselves, but they received us warmly and we prayed with them. They were very happy to meet us Jews but worried that the cost of living was going up because of us and that the local population's resentment of the refugees would also increase.

My father got work as a porter in a Russian orphanage and we moved into a nearby stable. Since his job was to carry bread from the bakery, we were not hungry. When the children from the orphanage lined up for soup, my little brother and I would stand with them. Later the staff refused to give us soup and there was less and less bread.

My brothers got work in a brick factory and my sister began to work as a corset-maker, but their wages were not enough to support us. I became friendly with the manager of a cooperative and every day he would sell me twenty kilos of bread, a package of tea, and a box of almonds. For a hundred-gram package of tea I paid him fifty rubles and sold it for sixty; for bread I doubled the price. One day a militiaman caught me carrying a package of almonds. During my interrogation the militiamen ate all the almonds, then they threw me out by the scruff of my neck. I stopped selling on the street, and customers would come to the stable, where we lived for a hundred rubles a month.

My father knew a warehouseman in a cooperative and we used to buy bread from him. We paid him thirty rubles a kilo and sold it for thirty-five or forty. Another warehouseman would sell us a little sugar, flour, and rice. The grown-ups would fetch the goods and the children would sell them. I was arrested ten times selling things on the tram and in the cinema. They beat me in the police station, but I did not give away our address and told them I was an orphan.

My father and I would stand on line all night in front of the cooperative for the flat cakes called *lepioshki,* which cost thirty kopecks apiece. We sold them for five rubles each. When the *lepioshki* ran out we sold soap, which my father's friend made in secret. I would deliver it to our customers. I risked getting arrested and, if caught twice, having my parents arrested. But I managed to dodge the police. After all that we still went hungry.

In Bukhara there were two oil mills that pressed rapeseed oil for the army. People used the pressed seeds to make oil cakes and sold them for two or three rubles each.

Among the officials at the Polish *delegatura*[*] in Bukhara we met someone we knew, and through him got an allowance of three hundred rubles a month.

---

[*]Office representing the Polish government-in-exile.

From the Polish *delegatura* in Bukhara we got two hundred rubles a month for the whole family and half a kilo of flour each. We were not given any clothes. Non-Jewish Poles got clothes and underwear.

In Kizduban there was a Polish outpost where every week we got a little flour and a few cans of food.

We children would get fifty rubles a month and a little food from the Polish *delegatura*. The highest pay for a factory worker was five rubles a day, while a loaf of bread on the black market cost a month's wages.

My father sent a letter to President Roosevelt asking him to help the refugees, and that very night he was arrested. Intervention by the Polish *delegatura* was of no help. While my father was in jail, my mother caught typhus and died.

In Djizak, 120 kilometers from Samarkand, there was terrible starvation, and by then we had nothing left to sell. We all got sick with typhus and were taken to the hospital, where my youngest brother died.

In Bukhara we lived in a stable and all of us got sick with typhus. My sister Esther died.

My seven-year-old cousin and I got sick with gastric typhus and were sent to the hospital together. She died in my arms.

We would stand for days and nights for four hundred grams of clayey bread. The Uzbeks would throw us off the lines and curse the Jews. After a few months my father died of starvation.

My father died in the night. In the morning Uzbeks came, scooped up his body, and drove away. They didn't allow me to drive with them, and I don't know where he is buried.

First my grandmother died of typhus, then my father, and we were left without anything to live on.

We slept in the train station because we had nowhere else to spend the night, and we all got sick with typhus. We recovered in the hospital, but then my father got pneumonia and died.

We slept out in the open and my parents caught cold. I tried in vain to get the hospital director to admit them. I managed to place them with an Uzbek but I had nothing for them to eat. They had a high temperature for three weeks. Finally I dragged them into a horse-drawn cab—no one helped me—and took them to the hospital. I left them in front of the building, just dropped them there and went back on foot. I was feeling sick, and I knew I had typhus.

After the amnesty was announced we thought we were saved. We didn't know that this stage would be the hardest.

It was much worse after the amnesty, when we arrived in Uzbekistan.

When we arrived in Samarkand it was harder for us than in exile.

In Samarkand our situation was worse than in the camp.

In Uzbekistan we realized how wrong we had been to leave the *posiolok*.

After the amnesty, when we arrived in Uzbekistan, we thought our end had come.

✿

We Knew We Were Dying

In Turkestan they held us at a train station eight kilometers from the town, and then the NKVD tried to send us all to a *kolkhoz*.

In Bukhara they would round people up, and anyone who could not produce proof of permanent employment was sent to a *kolkhoz*.

We slept on the streets, like thousands of other refugees. Many died on the street and there was no one to bury them. We were afraid we would die of hunger, and after a lot of trouble we managed to leave for Turkestan. But they would not let us off the train there and sent us off to the Burgen *kolkhoz*.

One day the NKVD announced that all Polish citizens should go to the train station, from where they would be sent to England. When we got there, armed guards surrounded us and we were taken in carts to a *kolkhoz*.

In Samarkand we had no roof over our heads and we were told to go to a *kolkhoz*.

In Samarkand we couldn't find a place to sleep and spent two weeks at the station. When my father went to Djambul to look for a place to stay, we were taken away to a *kolkhoz*.

We went to Leninabad but no one would take us in, so we wandered through the streets. Finally we went to the NKVD ourselves so as to be sent to a *kolkhoz*.

When my mother got out of the hospital we went to the *delegatura* for assistance, and spent the whole night on the steps in order to get inside. We got an allowance of only fifteen rubles, so, realizing that we would die of hunger, we went to the NKVD to be sent to a *kolkhoz*.

We were starving, although my father ran around the markets all day looking for a chance to make some money. He started selling candy, but was caught and put in jail for speculation. Since we were facing starvation, my mother put her name down to go to the *kolkhoz* with us.

We slept at the station. When we had nothing left to sell we went to a *kolkhoz*.

In Tashkent we slept out in the open, but in the end we had to go to a *kolkhoz*.

In Turkestan it was impossible to get bread and we had to go to a *kolkhoz*.

In Shakhrisabz we wandered around the streets, where refugees were lying side by side. So we went to a *kolkhoz*.

In Samarkand we lived on the street for a month, then went to the Voroshilov *kolkhoz*.

In Fergana we had nowhere to go, and in her arms Mama was carrying my little sister Sabinka, who had been born in Siberia, so we went to a *kolkhoz*. We slept on boards in a *kibitka** and were hungry every day.

We were taken by force to the Janko Tarmash *kolkhoz*, not far from Bukhara. We lived in a mud hut and slept on the bare earth. In the beginning we worked and got four hundred grams of flour, but later there was no more work and we got nothing. We lived on grass and roots.

My mother, both my sisters, and my youngest brother were sent to one *kolkhoz* and my father, my other brothers, and I to another one called Telmann. We worked in the fields picking peanuts. We sewed ourselves big pockets that we stuffed with peanuts, and that is how we survived.

We had to go to a *kolkhoz* called Uzbek. We worked hard, and we would have died of hunger if I hadn't stolen some rye every day.

When we left the hospital we had to go to a *kolkhoz,* and we worked in the cotton fields. When we were so weak that

---

*Nomad's tent; here used to mean a mud hut.

we couldn't work, we were given no bread. We sold our last pillow and our last shirt—we were ragged and naked.

We went to the Utro *kolholz*. My father worked in the fields, and we picked cotton. My father would get a kilo of rye, and we half a kilo each. Mama would grind it and bake flat cakes. Later on, the rye rations were reduced.

We were moved to a *kolkhoz* beyond Krasnogvardyeisk. Mama would go into the fields to pick radishes, and for that she got soup twice a day. I couldn't stand the taste of that soup, so Mama would bake me radishes in the ashes that the Kazakhs left in the fields. The Kazakhs used to cook some sort of wild plants in huge pots and then eat them with their hands. There wasn't a single spoon in the whole *kolkhoz*.

In the *kolkhoz* there were a thousand Uzbeks and five hundred refugees from Poland. The Uzbeks ate pretty well but wore rags, lived in windowless *kibitkas*, slept on the ground, and did not know what furniture was. Hersh and I dug potatoes and my father picked cotton.

The Kizyl-Yuldus *kolkhoz* was ten kilometers from Tashkent. We worked picking cotton for four hundred grams of flour, which I used to make into noodles with watery soup, and that was our morning and evening meal. The mud huts dripped water when it rained, and we were literally living in mud.

In the Pyatilyetka *kolkhoz* my father, mother, and older sisters worked in the cotton fields, for which our family would get a kilo of flour.

In the Urtak *kolkhoz* we got two hundred grams of bread a day.

I stripped a thousand meters of cotton stems a day and got paid half a kilo of rye flour.

We all worked in the fields and got four hundred grams of grain a day each.

My brother and sister worked in the fields and got two hundred grams of flour a day, but there were days when they got nothing.

At the Intala *kolkhoz* my father said he was a shoemaker. They were very happy to have him and he immediately sat down to work, for which we got a handful of wheat each.

People got six hundred grams of bread for field work. As nonworkers my mother and I got three hundred. The locals had nothing in their huts apart from plank beds. The refugees slept on the ground.

We lived in a *kibitka* and all three of us worked in the fields, for which we got 250 grams of grain.

We lived in a *kibitka* and slept on a wet mud floor. Everyone worked in the fields, for which we got a little grain that Mama made into soup.

At the Maxim Gorky *kolkhoz* we worked in the cotton fields from morning till night for four hundred grams of flour. We lived in *kibitkas* together with Uzbeks, who were there to keep an eye on us and prevent any rebelling.

In the *kolkhoz* we worked in the cotton fields together with Mama, for which we got *lepioshki* and sometimes a hundred grams of flour. We were terribly hungry. The Uzbeks taunted us as "Jewish squires" and threatened to throw us out of the *kolkhoz*. Mama had to beg them to let us stay.

The *kolkhoz* was called Dimitrov, and it was worse than the *posiolok*. We worked in the cotton fields for two hundred grams of grain. Even young children worked. The day we were given a bit of rye flour was a great occasion for us. After a few weeks the Uzbeks announced they could no longer keep us because they had no food for us, but we begged them, and they let us stay a little longer.

Our group was sent to the Molotov *kolkhoz*, where for the first two days they gave everyone two hundred grams of flour, and later only one hundred. Everyone got sick with typhus.

They took us in a camel-drawn cart to the International *kolkhoz*, where my father immediately got sick.

In the Telmann *kolkhoz* we lived in a *chaikhana** with other refugees, most of whom had typhus, dysentery, and other diseases. They refused to take them to hospital and most of them died as they lay next to us.

In the Molotov *kolkhoz* there were nine Jewish families and

---

*Central Asian tea-drinking establishment.

one Polish—the rest were Uzbeks. In the beginning we got half a kilo of bread a day, but then came many days of nothing. The Uzbeks themselves were in a terrible situation. We worked hard in the fields. I was twelve and my hands were gashed and swollen from picking cotton. Later on we were moved to the Lenin *kolkhoz*, where it was even worse because they put us in a little room with twenty-five other people, all of them sick with typhus. Fortunately, we managed to get a separate wooden shack. The epidemic was very bad, and only half survived. Out of the Rotman family of seven, four died of typhus, and everyone in the Polish family died. When we were hungry we ate grass, which my mother made into "cutlets." We didn't even have salt to put in them, and we became swollen from that food.

When I got sick and was taken to the hospital, my little brothers, Abram and Zvi, had nothing to eat for several days and ran crying to the chairman of the *kolkhoz*. He gave them each a *lepioshka*, saying, "Whoever doesn't work doesn't eat." When I left the hospital I had fourteen days of sick leave coming to me, but they refused to give me my flour ration, so after a few days I had to go back to work. Even five-year-old Zvi had to work. I kept him close by me in the field and made sure he was busy when the overseer approached.

Mama was so weakened that she couldn't work. My brother and I worked picking cotton, and at first we got four hundred grams of flour each. Then the rations were reduced to two hundred grams, and we ate wild plants that made us ill.

The situation in the *kolkhoz* got worse and worse. Mama and my older sister became ill with dysentery and were taken to the hospital.

After great effort we were allowed to move to the *kolkhoz* where Mama was, but by then my father could hardly stand on his feet. Mama sold the last shirt for a little rice to keep him going, but he could no longer eat, and in March of 1942 he died. On the same day Lejbowicz from Rozwadów died, and we buried them both in the Russian cemetery, because there was no other.

In the First of May *kolkhoz* we spent three months in a

cold mud hut and received a handful of grain for a day's work. My little cousin died there of hunger. Later we returned to Bukhara, where our whole family came down with typhus.

We lived in a mud hut and worked harvesting grain. During harvesttime we got a kilo of rye a day but afterward the ration dropped by half, and then to three hundred grams. We all came down with typhus. After we got out of the hospital we didn't want to return to the countryside.

When I got out of the hospital I decided I'd rather die on the street than go back to the *kolkhoz*.

In the Molotov *kolkhoz* we lived in a *kibitka* and worked picking cotton for four hundred grams of bread. Then the bread rations were reduced so much that we had to go back to Samarkand.

In the *kolkhoz* we all worked in the cotton fields, for which we got 250 grams of grain. We ground it with stones and Mama made it into soups. Seeing that we would die of hunger, we went back to town. Mama caught malaria and was put in the hospital, and we drifted around living off wild plants.

First my father got sick, then all of us. Mama did not want to let us go to the hospital; she said they poisoned people there. We stayed in the *kibitka*, where there was no one to even give us water because Mama was working in the fields. God helped us and we got better, but they would not keep convalescents in the *kolkhoz*, so we returned to Tashkent.

We got out of the hospital but we were so weakened that we couldn't work or make a living. We went back to town, where we slept on the street. My mother and sister tried to bring our old clothes from Tashkent and sell them, but they were always searching and arresting people on the trains.

In the *kolkhoz* I plowed the land, wearing out my last pair of shoes in the process, and only got a kilo of flour for ten days' work. I quit the job and went back to town.

The Uzbeks chased us out of the *kolkhoz*, saying they had nothing to eat themselves, so we returned to Samarkand. My mother developed heart disease and couldn't move. We ran from house to house asking people to take her in. Finally we found a home for the disabled, and cried for so long that one of the people in charge took pity and admitted her.

I caught malaria and consumption in the *kolkhoz*. My father, seeing that I wouldn't last long, went back with me to town and started to buy and sell. He was making pretty good money but was spending it all on the doctor and medicine for me. Two thousand rubles was what my illness cost. I could see that my father was denying himself a piece of bread, giving everything to me.

When we got sick with typhus we were taken to the hospital. Mama and my brother Meir stayed there for ten days, and I for two months. When my temperature dropped my brother visited me and I begged him to bring little Sabinka to see me because I missed her very much, but the doctor would not allow it and because of that I got a fever again. I was moved to another hospital, where they wouldn't give me a blanket despite the cold, so my father went back to the first hospital to get my blanket and became infected with typhus. He was in the hospital for seven days, but when Mama came to see him on the eighth day he was no longer there. She didn't want to tell us, but when she picked me up from the hospital I could tell from her face that something had happened. When little Sabinka got sick with dysentery Mama was allowed to stay with her in hospital, and I remained with my brother in the *kolkhoz*. Because we were not working we were given nothing to eat, and we were dying of hunger. One day Mama said that Sabinka would not last long. When my brother and I went to the hospital, we saw Mama, and beside her two men with shovels. I was very frightened of those people with shovels, but I went up to Mama because I didn't want her to stand there alone. I was given Sabinka's little dresses and Mama went away with those people. I wept bitterly, because I loved my little sister more than anything in the world. When Mama came back home she was in despair and couldn't work anymore.

My brother dragged himself home from work and lay down on the floor. I went to the doctor's every day but could never catch him in. Finally after eight days I found him, and he sent my brother to a hospital twenty-five kilometers from the *kolkhoz*. Two days later I went to find out how my brother was feeling. They told me he had died in the night. I sat in front of the hospital all day waiting to take my brother's body to the cemetery. In the evening they told me that the funeral had already taken place, but they refused to show me where the grave was.

My father was bedridden. The *kolkhoz* was poor and we had nothing to feed him. Then he was taken to the hospital and I never saw him again. I don't even know where he's buried.

My brothers, Shloime, who was about twenty, and Aaron, about eighteen, stayed in bed for five days. Shloime died on the way to the hospital and Aaron in the hospital. We knew we were dying, so we left the *kolkhoz* and went back to town. We carried bricks in a brickyard and earned two rubles and three hundred grams of bread a day each.

We left the *kolkhoz* and moved to Krasnogvardyeisk, where we spent most of what my father earned on rent. Mama used to make us dumplings out of flour mixed with chaff, which pricked my tongue when I ate. Papa swelled up and his whole body became covered with sores that oozed pus, each drop of which made a new blister. His shirt was soaked with pus and blood. Then Mama became sick. She didn't cry or groan, just collapsed onto the bed and couldn't get up, so then I was the one who had to squeeze my father's sores. Papa told me to go into town and bring something to save Mama. I bartered his clothes for a bottle of milk and a little jam and tried to force the food into her mouth, but she clenched her teeth and refused to eat anything, and at one point shook her head so violently that I spilled the milk. I saw her fall asleep in such a strange way and then become as hard as stone. Papa said Mama had gone to sleep. For four days I sat by her and guarded her. Then some strangers came and took her somewhere. A Russian woman wanted to take me in but I didn't want to leave my Papa alone. A few days later he slid off his straw mattress onto the floor. I tried to drag him back but he was very heavy. Each arm weighed a *pood*.* I shouted to him but he didn't answer, even though his eyes were open. His

---

*Russian unit of weight equal to about thirty-six pounds.

eyes had always been blue but now they were a completely different color and tears were running from them. I began to weep loudly. A neighbor ran in and tried to reassure me, saying that he was asleep, but I wouldn't believe her and cried that we had to bury him. There was no money for a funeral. The neighbor's husband dug a hole and I helped him.

The first victim of dysentery was my ten-year-old brother Sender, who was taken to the hospital only after eight days had passed. By paying a large sum of money we got his body back, and we buried him in the Jewish cemetery. Three weeks later Mama got sick. We managed to get her into the hospital, but the following day she died. We wanted to bury her but were told that her body had been buried during the night in an unknown place.

My five-year-old brother Zissel got sick and my father managed to get him admitted to the hospital. I went every day to find out how he was. One day I found his little bed empty. I got my father. They told us he had died and had been buried but they refused to show us his grave.

My father got a job with the *delegatura* but soon got sick with dysentery and died. Then my mother died of the same disease. When I came back from her funeral the Uzbek wouldn't let me into the house, and I slept on the street.

My father got typhus, then my mother, my brother, my sister, and I got it too. As one of us left the hospital, another one went in. After the typhus my mother got dysentery, became terribly thin, and died. My father did not suffer for long and died after a few days.

We got over the typhus, but my father and mother were very weakened by the disease and I had nothing for them to eat. A Pole, an engineer who lived nearby, did a lot to help us. He stood on line for bread for us and sold a pair of my father's shoes to buy us something to eat. My father was forty-two, my mother forty-one. I sold their clothes to bury them in the Jewish cemetery in Bukhara, and I had a gravestone erected for them.

My mother got sick with malaria and lay on the wet floor. It was several days before she was taken to the hospital. My father came back very sad and wouldn't tell us how Mama was. It turned out she had died on the way, and instead of taking her to the hospital he had taken her to the cemetery. After my mother's death we ate wild plants until my father got sick. I begged them to no avail to take him to the hospital, and after eight days he died.

My father and mother got sick with typhus. They refused to give us a cart to take them to the hospital. They died on the same day. We cried all night and the next day buried them ourselves.

The situation in the town was getting worse and worse, because people were fleeing the *kolkhozes* in droves. They were dying on the streets and the corpses were being thrown into the garbage boxes. The most terrible disease was dysentery. People said it was caused by the oil cakes. A doctor would come from the Polish *delegatura* but he could do nothing, since you couldn't get medicine anywhere.

There were no doctors because they had all been mobilized for the front, and the hospitals only had dentists. One day I came to the hospital and asked my sister how our mother was feeling, and my sister said, "Say a prayer for our father." When I returned home after saying the prayer I found out that our mother too had died. We sewed a shroud from the sheets and sold things to pay the 150 rubles for a place in the Jewish cementery.

My father and mother got hunger spasms, but they refused to take them to the hospital. By the time they took them it was too late—my mother died the next day and my father two days later. I don't know where they are buried. Dina and I got sick with dysentery and were taken to the hospital. After a few days Dina died.

In Kazakhstan we all got sick with typhus, and after eleven days Mama died. My eldest brother, who was nineteen, also died. I went with my sick father and last remaining brother to the Frunze area, because we heard you could get more food there. My father got sick with dysentery there and after eight days died in the hospital. Only my brother and I remained out of the entire family.

We were so famished after the typhus that we gorged ourselves on grass and roots and we all got sick with dysentery.
First to die was my grandmother, who was sixty. That same
night my grandfather died. Before the eight days of mourning
had passed my father died, and two weeks after him, Mama.
After that, my uncle and his twenty-year-old wife.

My oldest brother Abram, who was eighteen, died of gal-
loping tuberculosis. We were not allowed to bury him proper-
ly, and people later saw dogs pulling his bones out. Three-
year-old Zissel died of brain fever like our mother, and our
youngest, Beniek, who was born in prison, froze to death.
Half our family died in Frunze.

Typhus and dysentery caused terrible devastation among
the refugees. Within a short time my grandfather, grandmother, aunt and her child and husband all died. After I was admitted to the Polish children's home I learned that my aunt's second child had died too.

Seven of us left Poland. Three died of hunger and diseases.

There were seven of us, and only my twelve-year-old
brother Abram and I remained.

Eleven of us had left for Russia, and only my two aunts,
three-year-old cousin, and I remained.

Of the fifteen people in our family exiled to Russia, six
remained. It was the same in other families.

When the news came that a Polish army was being formed,
my older brother and Uncle Meir went to Samarkand, but
they were not accepted. My uncle was in despair and died of
starvation, and after him his son Motl.

My father wanted to join the Polish army, but they
wouldn't accept him.

My father tried to join the Polish army as a driver, but they
wouldn't accept him because he was a Jew.

My older brother volunteered for the Polish army but as a
Jew he was not accepted.

I traveled to Tashkent, where a Polish army was being

formed. They were happy to accept Polish women for the female detachments but not Jewish women.

Many people wanted to go to jail because there they were fed and had a roof over their heads, but the Russians quickly noticed the trick and began issuing acquittals.

❖

Orphans

The Polish government set up 139 orphanages for refugee children, including some especially for Jewish children, but only a small number of the thousands of Jewish orphans and semiorphans found shelter there. Some of the Jewish children pretended they were ethnic Poles in order to be admitted.

Polish prime minister Sikorski told Stalin he wanted to evacuate the Polish army to Iran for training and in order to restore his soldiers (mostly former prisoners) to health. After bitter arguments, Stalin agreed to the evacuation of about 25,000 Polish soldiers to Iran as reinforcements for the British forces in the Middle East. At the same time, preparations were made to evacuate Polish orphans as well. The evacuation began in March 1942. About 33,000 soldiers were evacuated, taking with them some 11,000 civilians, including more than 3,000 children. A camp was set up for the evacuees in the Iranian port city of Pahlevi. On July 8, 1942, the Soviet deputy foreign minister, Andrei Vishinsky, informed the Polish ambassador that the entire Anders Army had permission to leave the Soviet Union. Ten days later, Churchill asked Stalin's permission to evacuate Polish civilians also. At a Polish–Soviet military conference on July 31, it was agreed that the number of evacuees would not exceed 70,000. Children from the orphanages, who numbered some 15,000, were in the first wave to leave, among them about 1,000 Jewish orphans. One evacuation route led through Krasnovodsk, and another through Ashkhabad and Mashhad.

A camp for 24,000 evacuated Polish citizens was set up in Tehran and a separate Jewish camp within it. The Jews established there an orphanage for Jewish children and took care of their health and education with the help of the Jewish Agency in Tehran. After fruitless efforts to transport the children to Palestine through Iraq or by air, the Jewish Agency

decided to transfer them by sea. In January 1943 the children were taken
by trucks to Bandar Shahpour on the Persian Gulf and from there by
freighter to Karachi, in what is today Pakistan. From Karachi, the chil-
dren sailed around the Arabian Peninsula and through the Red Sea to
the Egyptian city of Suez, where they boarded a train to cross the Sinai
Desert. On February 18, 1943, they arrived in Atlit, in northern Pales-
tine. A second transport came to Palestine overland in August 1943, after
the British put down a pro-German uprising in Iraq.

My father got bleeding dysentery, but they would not admit him to the hospital and he died the next day. Two weeks later when my mother and older brother were working in the fields, my little sister Feiga died in my arms. Fearing the terrible shock to my mother, we carried her out into a field and buried her. I feel numb in the legs when I remember how desperate our mother was when she found out. When she got sick with typhus, we managed to beg a cart from the *kolkhoz* chairman to take her to the hospital, but she died on the way. We took her back and buried her next to our father and Feiga. When my younger brother Hershel got sick I didn't want to take him anywhere, and a few days later we dug a fourth grave. Then my older brother and I sold all our things and left the *kolkhoz*. At the Kitab station, all our money was stolen while we waited for the train to Shakhrisabz. In Shakhrisabz we went to the Polish mission, where they gave us blankets at once, and the following day we were taken to the orphanage.

I sold my late parents' things in the *kolkhoz* and went to Shakhrisabz, where I applied to the Polish *delegatura* as a "complete" orphan—one who had lost both parents. They gave me a coat, shoes, and two blankets and told me an orphanage would be opening in a few days. An official at the *delegatura*, a Jewish woman, showed an interest in me. She asked me how much money I had and whether I had any relatives, and suggested I move in with her. She was nice to me and took a little money from me each day. When my money ran out, she began to beat me and chase me out of the house whenever men came to see her. Then she accused me of stealing and threw me out on the street, without even letting me take the coat and blankets I had gotten from the *delegatura*. I ran crying to the director. He gave me another coat and sent me to Kazan.

First my twenty-one-year-old cousin Eliezer got sick with dysentery and died a few days later. Then my mother got sick, and after her my brother Itzhak. They all died in the hospital. We didn't want to put our father into the hospital, but when his condition became serious we did. We buried my mother and cousin in the Jewish cemetery in Bukhara, but where my brother and father are buried I don't know, because the hospital didn't give us the bodies. After that, my deaf-mute sister was taken to a Russian orphanage and I was sent to the Polish one.

My father got pneumonia. Mama begged in vain for a doctor, and my father went out like a light. Mama washed him and wrapped him in a sheet, but no prayers were said for him because there was no one to do it. After Mama got sick with typhus and was taken to the hospital, I would get four hundred grams of black flour from the *kolkhoz* and learned how to bake flat cakes on hot bricks. Later I was taken to the Polish orphanage.

They concealed from us that our father had died in Bukhara. We were told that he had gone to look for work. Then our mother got seriously ill and they didn't give us anything to eat. The chairman of the *kolkhoz* told us to look for another place. We hunted for dogs and ate grass. Finally, we left the *kolkhoz* and went on foot to Samarkand. There our mother was admitted to the hospital and we went to the Polish *delegatura* and told them we were orphans. We were taken with the orphanage to Zyrbuliak near Kermine, where the Polish army was stationed. Malaria and dysentery were rampant, but the situation gradually improved.

My father and youngest brother got sick with typhus, but there was no cart to take them to the hospital and they lay with us on the floor. We had nothing to cover them with, and after a few days they died. The Uzbeks did not allow us to bury them. They took the bodies away and we don't know what they did with them. Mama didn't want to stay in the *kolkhoz* anymore and we went to Turkestan, where after much trying she managed to get us into the Polish orphanage.

Since there was no work for us in the *kolkhoz*, we went to Tashkent. On the way my mother and brother both got sick and died. I went to the orphanage.

In Tashkent it was difficult to get food, even for money, and my father died of starvation. My mother got sick and also died. My twelve-year-old brother Abram and I returned to Bukhara, where we were accepted by the orphanage.

My father and mother were taken to the hospital. After eleven days my mother died and then my father. My little sister and I managed to get into the Polish orphanage.

My father was taken in by a prominent citizen of Bukhara, who had something like an apartment, and my mother slept in the synagogue. We were terribly hungry. My mother got sick with dysentery from eating potato peel, and died in the hospital. A month later my father died of typhus. I stayed with the Bukharan Jew and wept for days on end, searching for someone from Tomaszów or anyone who had known my father. I was lucky and met Mrs. Glancer from our town. She took me in, registered me on her passport, and got money for me from the Polish *delegatura*, which I could use to buy food. And besides, people receiving an allowance from the *delegatura* were not deported from the city.

Mrs. Jakubowicz from Łódź registered me as her son, and that way I got a bread ration card. Mrs. Jakubowicz worked in a shoe factory and thanks to her I got work there. One day she told me she was going to Yangi-Yulu in order to leave Russia with the Poles. I begged her to take me with her, but she said it would be difficult to get permission for two. I sold my shoes, tied up my feet with rags, and with the money I had made traveled to Yangi-Yulu. There I found Mrs. Jakubowicz and got onto the Jewish list together with her. When it turned out they were not taking Jews, Mrs. Jakubowicz returned to the factory and I remained alone in Yangi-Yulu. I was dying of hunger. I begged a piece of bread from a Polish soldier on guard duty. When I told him my story he interceded on my behalf and I was accepted by the Polish orphanage.

I missed my mother and for days would sit in the hospital courtyard and at night creep inside and sleep on the floor. A woman doctor found me there, took care of me, and tried to pull strings with the Polish *delegatura* to get me out of Russia.

I walked from the *kolkhoz* to the Polish orphanage near Samarkand. I walked barefoot through the snow. The director took pity on me and accepted me. From there I often went to Samarkand to look for my brother and his family, but I never found them.

I sold a few rags and rented a cubbyhole, but at night the young Uzbek whose house it was tried to force his way in, so I went to the orphanage. Many children envied me for being a "complete" orphan.

When out of our whole family only my brother and I were left, I went with him to Turkestan, where we were accepted by the orphanage.

When I was left alone in the world I was taken to the Polish orphanage.

After our parents died, my brother and sister tried to get me into the Polish orphanage in Turkestan, and after much effort they succeeded.

All three of us went to the Polish orphanage and begged them until they took us in.

We went to the Polish orphanage, twenty kilometers from the place where we had lost our parents.

When my mother died, my father managed after much effort to get me and my brother into the Polish orphanage. Both our sisters remained with him in Bukhara, and we never saw them again.

After Mama died my father put us in the Polish orphanage.

After my father died Mama pressured the orphanage until they accepted me.

Mama managed to get my sister and me into the Polish orphanage.

Mama put the four of us in an orphanage. Our oldest brother stayed with her.

When she got out of the hospital, Mama went to the *delegatura* and begged them until they accepted my younger brothers in the orphanage. Later our situation became so terrible that Mama had to put me in the orphanage as well. I didn't want to leave her, but there was no other choice.

My father went with me to Tashkent and put me in a Russian orphanage. There were a lot of ruffians there who used to call me Jew and beat me up. I cried to be let out, but the teacher refused, so in the night I dug a tunnel under the fence and escaped. On my way a vicious dog attacked me and bit me terribly. In the hospital I didn't tell them where I had escaped from, and they took me to the Polish orphanage.

My father managed to get me into a Russian orphanage where there were many Polish children.

From the hospital we were taken to an orphanage where out of a hundred Polish children there were twelve Jews.

My father went into town and kept trying until he finally managed to get my sister, brother, and me into an orphanage that had only Jewish children.

When my father was in the hospital, my cousin, whose wife had died in Komi, told him that he had put his children in a Polish orphanage in Djalabad and that two of them were going with the Poles to Tehran. My father asked him to get us in there too, but my cousin said they only accepted orphans. I took my younger sisters and we traveled to Djalabad. We stood weeping in front of the orphanage for several days. They didn't believe us, and gave us candy and toys to get us to tell where our parents were, but we kept insisting they were dead and finally we were accepted.

My brother and I got sick with dysentery, and from the hospital the Polish *delegatura* took us to the children's home.

My younger brother Moishele got sick with tuberculosis and the Polish *delegatura* sent him to a sanatorium. After a couple of months he was taken from there to an orphanage.

When a Polish children's home was opened in Kermine my father managed to get the three of us accepted there.

When they heard there was a Polish children's home in Kattakurgan my parents managed to get my brother and me into it. They themselves moved to a nearby *kolkhoz* so they could come and see us.

When a Polish children's home was opened in Samarkand my father got a job there and got me in.

When the Polish mission was opened to help the refugees, Mama pulled strings to get a job as a cook in the orphanage, which was designated for four hundred Jewish children. That orphanage was treated worse than the others: it was given potatoes less often and only dark flour, which Mama made into noodle-and-water soup, but even so we felt lucky because we had something to eat.

When Mama heard there was a Polish children's home in Karasu, she went there with us. My older brother Moishe did not want to leave Mama all alone and went back to the *kolkhoz* with her. I never saw them again.

They didn't give us much to eat in the children's home. Anyone who wanted to would go into town to look for food. Whole groups of Polish children would set off for the orchards and pick unripe fruit. Many children got sick and died.

Every day four or five children died. Eighty died within a few weeks.

I got typhus and pneumonia in the children's home and spent several months in the hospital. Mama left the *kolkhoz* and moved into a stable in Samarkand so she could visit me.

After six weeks in the children's home my brother got dysentery. Every day my mother would take *lepioshki* to him in the hospital, where they didn't give him enough food. His condition improved quickly and my mother thought she would be able to take him out of the hospital in a few days. One day she arrived and saw with horror another child in his bed. They told her that he had died suddenly and had been buried. My mother fainted and, when she came round, started shrieking that they had killed her child. They even refused to show her where he was buried. After my brother died, my father tried to get me out of the children's home, but he couldn't.

My father would not allow me to go to the children's home, but I was so starved that I didn't listen to him. I told them I was an orphan and was accepted. I would come back home at night, so my father didn't find out.

My mother tried to get us into the Polish children's home, but each time they told her there was no room. After much crying and begging, they gave her authorization for us to be admitted to a reformatory. We were accepted—my eleven-year-old sister Tsila, my nine-year-old brother Yehoshua, and I. There was no shortage of food, but we were not allowed to speak Yiddish.

The Polish children's home didn't accept fourteen-year-olds. I said I was ten and that both my parents were dead.

Mrs. Glancer found out that only children who had lost both parents were accepted in Kazan, and we went there. They wouldn't take me, but I showed them the papers proving that my parents were dead and that my father had been a rabbi, and was accepted. I was the only Jewish child in the orphanage, and during the five months I spent there I suffered quite a bit from the Polish children, although I was polite to everyone and never complained. One of the teachers always stood up for me.

After our parents died my brother and sister tried for a long time to get me into the Polish orphanage in Turkestan, and I was finally accepted. The Polish children treated me badly but the teacher took my side.

When I heard about the Polish orphanage in Kurkurovsk I went there with my sisters Miriam and Tsipora. We said we were orphans and cried for so long that they took us in. There was no shortage of food, but the Jewish children were forced to pray with the Polish ones.

I went with my little brother to the Polish orphanage and told them we had no father or mother. I cried for so long that they took us in. There was no shortage of food but we were forced to pray with the Polish children and to make the sign of the cross, which we were not willing to do. Only the very small children would do it.

I spent a year in a children's home. The Polish children bullied us a lot and we were forced to say Polish prayers—anyone who refused was beaten.

The Polish children would not let me pray and called me a dirty Jew.

In the children's home the Polish children called us dirty Jews.

We suffered a lot from the Polish children, who used to shout "Jews to Palestine!"

We were hungry in the orphanage too, but the worst thing was the Christian children calling us lousy Jews and teasing us that we would be sent to Palestine. One time I told them that I wasn't afraid of Palestine at all because it was my homeland.

The Polish children would get thick soup while we only got the watery part, and we were always hungry, even though the commission had recommended extra nutrition for us.

The Polish children were given three plates of soup each while we only got one, and watery at that.

We would get food and clothes, but the Polish children bullied us terribly.

There were only ten of us in a whole crowd of Christian children, who used to bully us terribly.

Out of three hundred Polish children there were twenty Jews. We were beaten and humiliated at every turn.

After Whitsuntide we were accepted in the Polish children's home, where out of 320 children there were twenty Jews. We would get 150 grams of bread a day and a little watery soup for lunch. The Polish children took out all their anger on us and said the Jews were to blame for everything. One day some Polish children found a torn holy picture and accused Reich and Rozenberg of having torn it. They were given such a beating that they had to stay in bed for several days. We were beaten too, and it was a long time before the director managed to calm the children down.

After much pleading I managed to get my youngest brothers, Abram and Zvi, into the Polish orphanage in Tashkent, but Abram escaped after a few days because the Polish children were beating and insulting him. Later on a Jewish woman became the director and we were all taken in.

After much effort I got into the Polish orphanage, where out of two hundred children there were fifty Jews, and I was treated well.

Out of a hundred Polish children in the orphanage there were twenty Jews, and we felt very good. The older boys were allowed to pray and the director, Mr. Franciszek, would not allow anyone to harm us.

The Polish children in the orphanage bullied us a great deal, but the teacher was a very kind woman and did not allow anyone to harm us.

I felt good in the orphanage. The director would not allow anyone to beat me or call me a dirty Jew.

The Polish children did bully us a lot, but the teachers were kind.

The Polish children often beat me up, but I didn't complain because not only was I eating my fill but also each evening I would take home a piece of bread, which enabled both of my sisters to survive. When my father asked me where I was all day and where I got the bread from I told him I was working for some Jew in Samarkand.

We would get four hundred grams of bread a day, but we were afraid our father would die of hunger, so my little brother and I would eat only half and give the rest to him so he wouldn't die.

We would get three hundred grams of bread day and a plate of soup. Part of the bread we would take to our older brothers and sisters, even though there was a severe penalty for that.

I would creep out of the orphanage and go to my mother with the bread I didn't eat. One day I found her in such a state that I didn't want to go back to the orphanage, but she would not let me stay.

The Polish children bullied us a lot, but we didn't care because a piece of bread and a little soup were the most important things for us. We saved the bread and gave it to our parents when they came to see us.

From time to time our parents paid us secret visits. We would each save a piece of bread and give it to them.

We had a bad time in the children's home and the Polish

children called us dirty Jews, but from time to time we would sneak out and take whatever we could to our parents.

The Polish children treated us badly but we accepted all the abuse, because we knew that by being there we made things easier for our parents.

The Polish children bullied us terribly, but we endured everything since we knew we couldn't go home.

When they told us we were going to Iran, we collected bread for our older brothers and sisters who had to stay behind in Bukhara. We were afraid the director would find the bread and accuse us of stealing, so we told her. She was not a kind woman and used to give the Polish children bigger rations of bread than the Jewish children, but she turned out to be sympathetic because we had told her the truth.

We were all hungry and dirty in the orphanage and everyone wanted to escape. When a convoy to India was organized everyone wanted to leave, but only thirty-five children were chosen, including three Jews.

When the list of children to be evacuated from Russia was drawn up, only ten Jewish children were on it. Our Jewish director tried in vain to intervene. Lots were drawn for who was to go and I got lucky, but ninety other Jewish children were left behind. My two brothers cried bitterly that they were not going. I said I would not be separated from them, but the director wanted me to leave and finally brought me a letter from my father, in which he wrote, "If I myself am not lucky enough to get to Palestine, then at least let me have the consolation that my son is there."

There were only four of us Jews in the children's home. When they were getting ready to leave we were informed that they were not taking us along. We cried bitterly and begged them to take us. One of the teachers had pity on us and took us to a little train station outside Kattakurgan, where we waited all day. When the train with the Polish children came in, she ran from car to car begging the people in charge to let us on. Finally we did get into one car, and left without any of our things and without saying good-bye to our parents.

Our orphanage was sixteen kilometers from town. When they told us we were going to Tehran we went to say good-bye to our parents. By the time we returned, the other children had already left for the station. Mama ran with us. The train was standing in the station but the director refused to let us on. The teacher begged him and he relented. We were so upset, we didn't even manage to say good-bye to Mama.

When they started registering children to leave the country, I went to the head of the *delegatura* and asked him to send me along with them. He said they were not taking Jews, but that he would see what he could do. I didn't say good-bye to my mother. I had seen her only once since going to the orphanage. I was afraid they would discover I was not a complete orphan and throw me out.

One day we found out that children in the orphanage where my brother Moishele was were to be evacuated to Persia. I went to the station, pretending I wanted to say good-bye to them. We exchanged caps and, with a Polish eagle on my beret, I boarded the train. I got as far as Kazan. There they checked the children and found out I did not belong there. I begged, but it was no use and they threw me off the train. A Polish soldier, seeing me crying, pushed me back onto the moving train at the last moment. Unfortunately for me, the head of the *delegatura* was traveling in that very car. He stopped the train and I had to return to Bukhara. Then, through a friend in the *delegatura*, my father begged a place for me in the Polish children's home. But only non-Jewish children were to be evacuated. At the last minute they decided to include four Jewish children, and I was among them.

On the day of our departure we got new sweaters. My youngest brother, Saul, took them to our parents, to sell for bread. On the way thugs attacked him and tried to take the sweaters. They beat him, but he refused to let go of the sweaters, because he knew this was the last thing we could do for our parents.

When it was time for the evacuation our parents came and asked us to stay, but we did not want to.

My father told us to return home because he did not want to be separated from us. I felt sorry for him, but I remembered how terribly hungry we had been and decided we wouldn't go back. They came to the assembly point. My stepmother was holding my baby sister in her arms. The baby stretched out her little hands to us, begging us to take her along. We were all in tears.

The first convoy consisted of ninety children, including fifteen Jews. I went with the second one, which had seven Jewish children. My brother Yehoshua got sick with dysentery and stayed behind.

We were taken to Ashkhabad with the third convoy. The first and second ones were for non-Jewish children.

My two brothers left while I stayed behind in Ashkhabad by the Persian border because I was sick.

From our orphanage, only ten children went to Persia, the ones like me who had lost both parents.

Out of forty children, they selected only eight, only those who had lost both parents.

The refugees who said good-bye to us at the station envied us for getting out of Russia.

Convoys were leaving all the time but my little sisters and I were not taken.

Three groups left, but none of them included Jewish children. A new convoy of 320 children was supposed to be taking twenty Jewish children.

After four months a group of children set off, but they did not send us with them and threatened to leave us in Russia for the slightest misdemeanor.

Several times, groups would leave, but we didn't want to go with them because we had heard that parents would also be evacuated. We left with the last convoy when we learned that the Bolsheviks weren't letting Jews out.

We found out that in addition to the military, distinguished rabbis could also leave Russia, so a delegation of rabbis went to Yangi-Yulu to see General Anders. The general promised to do as they asked, but only a few were allowed to leave, including my uncle.

My father spent whole days at the *delegatura* trying to

leave with the military convoys, but he was unsuccessful. They refused to take Jews. Even the wives of Jewish military had to remain in Russia.

In order to get my papers I arranged a marriage with a Polish soldier, and that is how I got out.

For four thousand rubles I arranged a marriage with a Polish soldier, and on August 7, 1942, I left for Tehran with the military families.

At the border the Russians took my gold wedding ring, the only souvenir of my late parents.

Since I have blond hair and don't look Jewish, I managed to get into the Polish children's home in Yangi-Yulu, and that's how I got out of Russia. I traveled to Krasnovodsk as the daughter of a Polish serviceman. I will never forget what he did for me.

Several convoys of children departed, but I was always left behind because I was Jewish. Finally I got sick with typhus and spent two months in the hospital. When I found out that the last convoy was leaving, I escaped from the hospital. Thanks to a teacher who was kind to me I managed to get to the convoy, and I left with the other children for Krasnovodsk.

The Polish children were taken to the station in carts, whereas we—seventy-two Jewish children—were ordered to go there on foot. When the Polish children had been loaded onto the train, the convoy leader said that the Jewish children were staying behind. We thought it was a joke and that they would take us in the end. When the train moved we began to weep bitterly. A priest, moved by our tears, told them to stop the train. He had a long talk with the convoy leader, until finally they shoved us into a car and we left for Krasnovodsk. We suffered a lot on the way, because they gave us no water to drink.

We stopped speaking Yiddish among ourselves so that no one on the train would know we were Jewish. When the train stopped in Bukhara, we saw Jewish children from the first convoy who had been taken off the train and abandoned to their fate. They were crying and begging to be taken with us. Some wanted to throw themselves under the train.

The children who arrived later said they had seen children throwing themselves under the trains when refused a place on the convoy.

We arrived by train in Krasnovodsk, where there was no water. For three days we drank seawater, which was salty and stank of kerosene.

We arrived in Krasnovodsk, where we were dying of thirst, and I used my last rubles to buy water. The water situation was no better on the ship.

Not all the children survived the journey to Krasnovodsk. A hundred children died on the way.

In Krasnovodsk we spent the night near the port. First they took the military onto the ship, then the children.

We arrived by train in Krasnovodsk, and from there a ship took us to Pahlevi.

We sailed on the *Kaganovich* to Pahlevi, where the Polish Red Cross was waiting for us.

We sailed from Krasnovodsk to Pahlevi, where we got new clothes.

We were taken in trucks to Bukhara, then to Kazan and Ashkhabad, where they washed us and gave us new clothes.

We were taken to Ashkhabad on the Iranian border.

I was sent to Ashkhabad, where out of three hundred Polish orphans there were twenty Jews.

In Ashkhabad the Polish children greeted us with cries of "The Jewish brats have arrived!"

In Ashkhabad a commisssion examined us. It found that five children were over sixteen and decided to send them back. Among them was my brother Hersh. We pleaded with the doctors in vain. The Polish children who were over sixteen were not sent back.

The Polish children beat us, made fun of us, spat in our faces, and stuffed soap into our mouths at night.

In our convoy there were 320 children but only twenty Jews. The Polish children bullied us, knocked our mess kits out of our hands, poured water into our beds, stuffed soap into our mouths, and beat us in the dark. The director could not control them. We put up with it all because we believed our suffering would soon be over. And anyway, the *kolkhoz* had been worse.

We were beaten, insulted, and humiliated at every turn, and for the slightest offense they threatened to leave us behind in Russia. Finally, after eight months, we were sent to Mashhad and from there to Tehran.

After four months we were sent from Ashkhabad to Tehran.

We spent six months in Ashkhabad, the older children in tents, the younger ones in barracks. Then the Polish army took us to Tehran.

I spent a year in Ashkhabad. We were fine there. We went to school and there was no shortage of food. But later, when the Polish army left, the Russians arrested the director and the teachers and wanted to close the orphanage.

There were three hundred Polish children and twenty Jews, and the Russians threatened to send us to different *kolkhozes*.

After relations between Poland and Russia were broken, we would only get four hundred grams of bread and some soup. The director left with the embassy staff, and NKVD men kept coming to close down the orphanage and send us to *kolkhozes*. The new director, Mr. Orłowski, kept delaying the deadline as much as he could. The NKVD men would carry out searches, looking for older boys. The director hid them in the cellar and only showed the younger children. When they asked where our parents were, we said we were orphans. When they tried to persuade us to take Soviet passports, we said we had fathers in the Polish army abroad and wanted to join them. We Jewish children pretended to be Christian, for fear that they would not let us out of Russia otherwise. The director forbade us to go outside, so that we would not be taken away.

After Polish–Soviet relations were broken, everyone from the age of sixteen was forced to take Soviet passports, and those who resisted were put in jail. In our children's home they arrested twenty-five teachers and mistreated them in jail, where many died. They would take our carts, food supplies, and clothes. They were planning to shut down the home and send us to *kolkhozes* and I didn't believe we would ever get out of Russia, but at the last moment, on July 21, 1943, we were put onto trucks and taken to Mashhad on the other side of the border.

When we found out about the death of General Sikorski, all the children wept bitterly, saying our father had died and we would perish without him. The mourning lasted eight days. We wore black armbands and the children wouldn't eat. The director and the teacher comforted us, saying that the Polish government in London would not abandon us and would do everything to get us out of there. Three weeks later we got the news that they were coming for us in the night to take us to a *kolkhoz*. We cried and decided we wouldn't go voluntarily. The director comforted us, saying that he would do everything to save us. When the NKVD appeared, the children barricaded themselves in. The NKVD men announced they would take us by force, but the director refused to be intimidated. The negotiations lasted all day, and the director went to various places to intervene. When he came back at night, the teachers were woken up and the typewriters started banging out lists of children. We didn't sleep all night. Time and again a child would run up to the teacher and kiss her hands to get her to tell us the news, but she would just repeat, "It'll be fine." It was morning before they told us we were leaving Russia. We jumped for joy, danced, sang—it's hard to describe that scene. We each got three blankets and a few sheets, shoes, sweaters, and other things. That night we went to bed in our clothes because we were supposed to get up very early, but no one slept. At four in the morning reveille was sounded—it was July 21, 1943. We got onto military trucks driven by Russians. At the border the Russians tried to take our things. Most of all they wanted our blankets, but we fought for every item and didn't allow them to take a thing. The search went on all day and it was close to evening before we got to Mashhad.

✧

In Mashhad, the Persian Jews took us in, fed us, and gave us presents, and the Jewish children went on separately to Tehran.

In Mashhad, the Persian Jews gave us a rousing welcome, fed us, and gave us presents, and on the fourth day trucks took the Jewish children to Tehran.

In Mashhad, the Persian Jews received us very well, and the Jewish children were sent to Tehran, while the Polish ones went to Africa.

In Mashhad, all the Polish children were accepted, but we were told they were sending us back to Russia. We were in despair, and we cried until a Polish officer, a Jew, came and assured us we would be going to Tehran.

In Pahlevi, the Persians were very hospitable. They gave us cakes and, most important of all, water.

In Pahlevi, we lived in a tent for three weeks and got wonderful food: bread, eggs, milk, cocoa, and cooked meals.

In Pahlevi, they kept us for many days out in the open before taking us to Tehran.

I stayed in a Polish camp in Pahlevi for four weeks before I was taken to Tehran.

I spent four weeks in a camp in Pahlevi. I was very weak and they had to give me special care.

In Pahlevi, a commission of English doctors examined us. When they saw me, one of the doctors said, "What have they sent us, children or corpses?" and I was sent to the English hospital.

I spent a month in an English sanatorium in Pahlevi before I was sent to Tehran.

In Pahlevi, the children were divided into healthy and sick, but we smuggled out four of the sick ones so that they could go with us to Palestine.

We traveled in large trucks across the mountains.

We traveled over high mountains and down into valleys. I saw a Russian truck lying smashed up. Near Tehran the water in the radiator ran out and we couldn't continue. Fortunately we had stopped near a Polish camp and military trucks picked us up.

We were in the last group of children allowed to leave Russia.

My brothers arrived in Tehran on the last convoy.

I left Russia on the last convoy of children to Iran.

In Tehran, we stayed in camp number 3, where we heard they were sending us to Africa. We feared another long journey but a representative of the Jewish Agency came and took three hundred children who were to be sent to Palestine.

In Tehran, at first Poles looked after us, then the Jewish Agency sent teachers who prepared us for life in Palestine.

In Tehran, at first I was in a mixed camp, and later on they moved me to a Jewish orphanage.

In Tehran, I went to camp number 2, which was under the care of the Jewish Agency.

In Tehran, I could barely stand on my feet and they sent me to an English sanatorium. From there I was taken to camp 1, for Polish children, and was later transferred to camp 2, for Jewish children, where to my great joy I met my younger brother Moishele.

In Tehran, I was put in an English orphanage, and when I got better they transferred me to a Jewish orphanage.

In Tehran, I had typhus and was in the hospital.

In Tehran, many children had gastric typhus.

We lived in a camp outside Tehran. Many children died in that camp, despite the care and attention.

In Tehran, the Polish children would throw stones at us and shout, "The Moishes have arrived!"

In Tehran, I lived with Polish children in camp 1; then I got into the orphanage run by the Jewish Agency. They fed us well but we went around in rags. Whenever clothes came from India and America they were first divided up among the Poles, then the less-good things were given to the Jews. From those less-good things the orphanage staff took the best for themselves, leaving the rags for the children. The whole time I was in Tehran I walked around in a nightshirt; only on the day before my departure did I get a torn dress.

They fed us well, but we were still wearing rags.

In Tehran, I spent seven months in a Jewish orphanage. School was only once a week and we weren't given any clothes. Only on the day before departure did we get clothes.

I was in Tehran for eight months and never got any money to send a letter to my father. They would take my letters away, promising to send them, but I never got a single answer. The Polish children, who were given postage stamps, would get answers from Russia.

From Tehran the Polish children went to India and the Jewish children to Palestine.

In January 1943 I was taken from Tehran to Palestine.

We were in Tehran until January 1943. In February we arrived in Palestine.

I left Tehran, and in February 1943 arrived in Palestine with Miriam and Tsipora.

After a few months we left Tehran, and arrived in Palestine in February 1943.

After three months we were sent from Tehran to Palestine.

After six months I left Tehran for Palestine.

I was in Tehran for several months, then came to Palestine with other Jewish children.

After eight months in Tehran I arrived in Palestine with both of my younger sisters.

I spent seven months in Tehran, and on August 28, 1943, I arrived in Palestine with a group of a hundred children.

On the fifteenth of August, 107 Jewish children from Poland were loaded onto trucks in Tehran and taken through Iraq as Christian children. On August 28, 1943, we arrived in Palestine.

I arrived with a group of 108 Jewish children who were taken on military trucks through Iraq to Palestine.

From Tehran I crossed India and then came to Palestine.

After eight months in Tehran I was taken to Karachi, and from there I made a long journey to Palestine.

My younger brother Moishele and I came through Karachi to Palestine.

I arrived in Palestine with my eleven-year-old brother Yosef. Our youngest brother Saul stayed in Tehran because he was seriously ill.

I was sick, and it was only in September 1943 that I was brought to Palestine. How delighted I was to find both of my younger brothers here.

When I left Russia my father was in prison under a six-year sentence for speculation. The last time I saw him he was on the street under escort, on the way to prison. He was unshaven and ragged. One day he sent me a tin spoon on which he had scratched the words: "Save me, I'm dying of hunger." In March I got a letter from my mother telling me to say *kaddish* for my father.

I didn't want to leave my father but I realized I was a burden to him. Before leaving I gave him my clothes and blankets. We cried a lot when we said good-bye. He told me to be a good Jew and not to forget him.

Mama was standing in the station when we left. How hard it was to leave her there, sick and alone in a foreign country.

My father remained alone in Samarkand.

Our father gave us a note for our relatives in Palestine, begging them to save him. When the truck set off he sank to the ground. I don't know what became of him.

We get letters from our father complaining of hunger. We sent him a parcel.

We got a letter from our mother. We have no news of our father.

We have no news of our parents or our older sister.

My sister, who was twenty, stayed in Turkestan and I have no news of her.

We didn't say good-bye to our father or mother, and we never saw them again.

We didn't see Mama because we weren't able to go out when they told us we were leaving.

I didn't say good-bye to my mother, because I was afraid they would find out I wasn't a complete orphan. What became of her later I don't know.

To this day I don't know whether my father is alive, or where he is.

Where my parents and brothers are I don't know.

I saw my mother die, then my father. They both died of hunger.

My brother got malaria and was left behind in Russia. Only my little sister Sara and I came to Palestine.

We were four children in our house but only I came to Palestine.

We were seven brothers and sisters. Only I survived.

Since leaving for Tehran I've had no news of my family, and I'm probably the only one who survived.

I had six brothers and three sisters. Five of us fled to the Bolsheviks, three went back to the Germans. Now I'm all alone.

Out of my whole family, only I made it to Palestine.

When I was left alone in the world I was brought to Palestine.

When people ask me where I'm from, I say—from iron.

❧

List of Testimonies

Testimony no. 31: Eliezer Haltman, age fifteen, from Izbica, Lublin province.

Testimony no. 32: Mordechaj (?)owszowicz, age nineteen, son of Chaim Izrael and Rachel, born in Iwa near Lida; lived in Nowogródek (street address Piłsudski 45).

Testimony no. 36: Cywia Elsan, age fifteen, daughter of Henoch and Pesia, born in the town of Kurzan (? probably Różan) near Łomża. Arrived in Palestine with her brother Nisan, age twelve.

Testimony no. 37: Judyta Patasz, age fifteen, daughter of Fiszel and Chaja from Goworowo near Łomża. Arrived in Palestine with a sister and two brothers.

Testimony no. 40: Chaim Dawid Cwibel, age sixteen, son of Jehoszua and Saba from Kraków (Dietlowska 36).

Testimony no. 50: Josef Hurwicz, son of Jehoszua and Sara from Wieliczka near Kraków. Arrived in Palestine with his eleven-year-old brother Mojsze.

Testimony no. 53: Mordechaj Szmulewicz, age fifteen, son of Izrael and Adela from Łódź (Piotrkowska 276).

Testimony no. 65: Josef Rozenberg, age fifteen, from Krzeszów, Lublin province.

Testimony no. 74: Nachum Teper, age fifteen, from Nachal (?) near Lwów.

Testimony no. 76: Mojsze Gliksberg, age seventeen, son of Szmuel Jakub and Judyta from Różan.

Testimony no. 77: Gitla Rabinowicz, age seventeen, daughter of Rabbi Jechiel of Biała, born in Siedlce.

Testimony no. 79: Boruch Flamenbaum, age fourteen, son of Abraham and Sara from Biłgoraj.

Testimony no. 83: Szymon Turner, age thirteen, son of Icchak and Lea from Osiany Dolne.

Testimony no. 88: Helena Ajzenberg, age twenty-five, from Warsaw.

Testimony no. 102: David Auschibel, age fourteen, son of Josef and Małka from Leżajsk.

Testimony no. 107: Jechoszua Frydman, age sixteen, son of Rabbi Abraham from Tomaszów Lubelski.

Testimony no. 108: Josef Barten, age fourteen, son of Wolf and Rebeka from Majdan Kołbuszewski.

Testimony no. 109: Izrael Ferster, age fifteen, son of Symcha and Gitla from Majdan Kołbuszewski. Arrived in Palestine with two sisters.

Testimony no. 110: Dina Stahl (should read Sztark), age eleven, daughter of Josef and Estera from Rabka.

Testimony no. 111: Lunia Akerman, age thirteen, from Warsaw; father had a clothing shop on Wołowa Street. Arrived in Palestine with an eight-year-old brother.

Testimony no. 112: Sima Siebcesser (should read Zibcener), age thirteen, daughter of Mendel and Rajzla from the village of Tarnówka near Łańcut.

Testimony no. 113: Eliezer Hochmeister, age fifteen, son of Dawid and Noemi, from Warsaw (Pawia 41).

Testimony no. 114: Eliezer Kreitner (should read Kretner), age thirteen, son of Bencjon and Elka from Małopolska (?).

Testimony no. 115: Luba Milgram, age twelve, from Kałuszyn near Warsaw.

Testimony no. 116: Mojsze Lipowicz, age eleven, son of Zelik and Rojza from Pułtusk.

Testimony no. 117: Chaim Cymerman, age thirteen, son of Michał and Perla from Hrubieszów. Arrived in Palestine with his sister Małka.

Testimony no. 118: Sara Mławer, age twelve, daughter of Michał and Rywka from Przasnysz. Arrived in Palestine with her brother.

Testimony no. 119: Estera Barasz, born in 1926, from the town of Lesko, near Sokal, Lwów province.

Testimony no. 120: Meir Szpalter, age fourteen, from Przeworsk.

Testimony no. 121: Zeev Frenkel, age fourteen, son of Rabbi Menasze and Miriam from Leżajsk.

Testimony no. 122: Frajda Celnikier, age eleven, daughter of Mojżesz and Noemi from Warsaw (Niska 35).

Testimony no. 123: Józef Wajdenfeld, age fourteen, from Bielsko.

Testimony no. 124: Saul Gliksberg, age fifteen, from Różan.

Testimony no. 127: Arie-Lejb Klajncaler, age fifteen, from Czarny Dunajec, Kraków province.

Testimony no. 131: Jakub Rabinowicz, age sixteen, son of Jechiel from Siedlce.

Testimony no. 132: Szoszana Elkes, age twelve, daughter of Josef and Chana from Pułtusk. Arrived in Palestine with three sisters and a brother.

Testimony no. 134: Judel Dembowicz, age thirteen, from Suwałki.

Testimony no. 135: Motel Gejer, age fifteen, from Łaszczów, Lublin province.

Testimony no. 136: Miriam Lipowicz, age thirteen, daughter of Zelik and Rojza from Pułtusk.

Testimony no. 140: Jakub Piwko, age twelve, son of Berisz and Hinda from Brok on the Bug.

Testimony no. 142: Cipora-Fela Enoch, age thirteen, from Bielsko.

Testimony no. 143: Chawa Wowerman, age ten, from Biała Podlaska.

Testimony no. 144: Miriam Krambajn, age thirteen, daughter of Natan and Dwojra from Łańcut. Arrived in Palestine with her eleven-year-old sister Chawa.

Testimony no. 151: Jafa Iras (should read Irom), age thirteen, daughter of Josef and Bracha from Zagórze in Galicia.

Testimony no. 152: Abram Elkan (should read Elkies), age eleven, son of Josef and Chana from Pułtusk.

Testimony no. 155: Alter Zajdman, age thirteen, from Kałuszyn.

Testimony no. 156: Gedali Niewiadomski, age thirteen, from Siedlce.

Testimony no. 157: Ida Bauminger, age fifteen, from Kraków.

Testimony no. 163: Rebeka Frenkel, age twenty-five, from Limanowa.

Testimony no. 165: Gita Wagszal, age fourteen, from Nowy Sącz.

Testimony no. 170: Ludwik Ferster, age sixteen, son of Józef and Pola from Warsaw (Koszykowa 39).

Testimony no. 171: Abram Frenkel, age sixteen, son of Rabbi Efraim from Mielec.

Testimony no. 172: Rut Lefler, age eighteen, daughter of Salomon and Waleria from Bielsko.

Testimony no. 175: Estera Barasz, age sixteen, from Lesko, near Lwów.

Testimony no. 176: Jakub Płoński, age sixteen, son of Manes and Tauba from Vilna.

Testimony no. 178: Ida Kowen, age seventeen, from Jarosław.

Testimony no. 181: Jósef Geller, age thirteen, son of Mordechaj and Miriam from Oświęcim.

Testimony no. 185: Guzel Zaf, age sixteen, son of Lejb and Rachela from Wyszków.

Testimony no. 186: Tauba Tuchsznajder, age thirteen, daughter of Zajnwil and Fryda from Chełm Lubelski. Arrived in Palestine with three sisters and a brother.

Testimony no. 186A: Hala Kirszbraun, age twelve, daughter of Dawid from Warsaw.

Testimony no. 187: Mojsze Sznal, age fourteen, son of Matiasz and Gitla from Tarnów.

Testimony no. 188: Abram Rozenband, age fourteen, son of Hipolit and Estera from Warsaw (Wolska 100).

Testimony no. 192: Sara Zylberfaden, age thirteen, daughter of Mordechaj and Rywka from Warsaw.

Testimony no. 195: Izrael Wajner, age thirteen, son of Josef and Chaja from Włodawa.

Testimony no. 196: Mojsze Szrajber, age thirteen, son of Pinchas and Lea from Rozwadów.

Testimony no. 200: Mojsze Sznajder, age thirteen, son of Jakub and Perla from Tomaszów Lubelski.

Testimony no. 204: Abram Rajf, age fourteen, from Krasnobród, Lublin province.

Testimony no. 210: Sara Broder, age twelve, from Pułtusk.

Testimony no. 214: Jakub Kalman, age seventeen, from Bochnia.

Testimony no. 240: Mojsze Grajcer, son of Dawid and Sara from Stoczek Lubelski.

Testimony no. 254: Miriam Kołdra, age sixteen, from Warsaw (Czerniakowska).

Testimony no. 302: Szlomo Beglikter, age eighteen, from Cologne.

Unnumbered testimony: Chaim Besser, born in 1927, son of Icchak and Miriam from Łuków, Lublin province.

❖

Afterword

ISRAEL GUTMAN

Jews in Palestine received only fragmentary and contradic- tory news from the Polish lands occupied by the German and Soviet armies—news that, while arousing profound anxi- ety, failed to convey the true horror of the situation. Every- thing indicated that it was the Jews who were the group most persecuted by Hitler's regime. That kind of experience, how- ever, was not rare in Jewish history. But no information reached Palestine about the mass murder of Jews by the so- called *Einsatzgruppen* following the German invasion of Sovi- et territories in 1941. The inhabitants of Palestine did not learn of that until the latter half of 1942, from reports trans- mitted to London by the Polish underground and from an official statement by the Polish government-in-exile. Only then did they begin to realize that this was no ordinary wave of pogroms but an enterprise aiming at the biological destruc- tion of the Jews in the occupied lands. However, psychologi- cal barriers prevented them from imagining a crime on such a scale.

The vastness of the crime was understood only in Novem- ber 1942, after a group of sixty-nine Jews arrived in Palestine, exchanged for Germans who had been held by the Allies. Mass demonstrations broke out, led by social, political, and religious organizations. The protests, hunger strikes, appeals, and mourning, however, had no influence on the actions of the Nazi criminals or on the operational plans of the Allies, or even on the policy of the British authorities in Palestine. Throughout the entire war these authorities maintained the limited immigration quota, and Jews who did manage to tear themselves from Hitler's clutches were viewed as citizens of an enemy country. In these conditions, illegal immigration almost completely stopped, especially once Palestine came under threat of invasion by General Rommel's troops from North Africa. The British authorities first rejected, then postponed the plan to send Jewish paratroopers from Palestine to the occupied countries. There were also delays in setting up a Jewish Brigade with the British armed forces. In this atmosphere of Jewish helplessness and powerlessness, the news that hundreds of Jewish children from Polish cities and towns had arrived aroused profound emotion among Palestinian Jews. These orphans became a symbol of the orphaned Jewish nation.

There was much bitterness and regret during the evacuation by General Anders's army, with which the children managed to get out of the Soviet Union. In the first phase of the evacuation, in April 1942, about 30,000 soldiers and 14,000 civilians left, including only 600 Jews in uniform and 300 civilians. It was said that Jews were deliberately barred from the convoys and were indeed taken off them. Following protests and pressure from Jewish organizations in many countries, during the next phase, in July 1942—when 40,000 soldiers and more than 25,000 civilians left Soviet Russia— 1,300 Jewish soldiers and 1,688 civilians, including 871 Jewish children, went with them.

After enduring a difficult journey to Krasnovodsk and the degrading living conditions in the Iranian port city of Pahlevi, the children reached Tehran in the second half of 1942. It was there, in civilian camp number 2, that a Jewish orphanage was set up. The teachers were people who had received some training from Zionist youth organizations. Later Tsipora Sharet, the wife of the later Israeli prime minister Moshe Sharet, arrived from Palestine and took over the running of the orphanage. After the lack of food, clothing, and sanitary supplies was dealt with, an effort was made to provide the children with schooling, cultural activities, entertainment, and, above all, an atmosphere based on respect for their dignity.

The last stage of their wandering, from Iran to Palestine, turned out to be more complicated than expected, since the Iraqi authorities refused permission for the transit of the Jewish children overland. The Americans were asked to provide air transport, but at the last minute American air communications with Tehran were broken. It was suggested that the Jewish children travel through Iraq as members of the Polish volunteer youth brigade, but the British objected to deceiving the Iraqi authorities. Nor did Egypt agree to the transit of Jewish children to Palestine. Finally they were loaded onto a ship taking British soldiers eastward, to India, and arrived in Karachi on January 23, 1943. Two weeks later they set off again in the opposite direction, and on February 17 they sailed into Suez.

A Jewish soldier serving in the Palestinian divisions of the British army in Suez described the event: "Throughout the whole night we prepared bags of sweets and the canteen was emptied clean. The most touching moment was when the children appeared singing a Hebrew song whose words say that we are all children of our mother."

On February 18, 1943, after more than three years of persecution, wandering, and exile, this crowd of emaciated, tormented children finally reached Palestine. The news sent a tremendous surge of emotion through the Jewish settlements. When the train carrying the children arrived in Rehovot, they were greeted at the station by thousands of people, among them delegations from schools, women's organizations, and the clergy. The children were enchanted by the exotic landscape and marveled at the aroma of oranges.

In each settlement they were greeted warmly and showered with gifts and love. Many social organizations, kibbutzim, and political and religious groups fought over the "Tehran children," arguing about where and in what kind of environment they should be raised. They were questioned about their family homes to determine whether they came from a religious or secular environment.

Today the "Tehran children" belong to varied strata of

Israeli society, but they still maintain active social contact and organize meetings. One of them who attended the 1993 reunion in Jerusalem to mark the fiftieth anniversary of the arrival of the convoy in Palestine said, "We've got grown-up children and grandchildren of our own now, but we will always remain the 'Tehran children.'"

✿

Jewish Lives